+ peripateticus ñ ut ph̄s pc

cxxiiii.

Marsilius ficinus Laurentio medici . / . magnanimo.

Oliuerius arduinus / insignem peripateticum comendare
t ñ mediocrit / in aristoteles suus cū t plurimū
comendaret. Si aristoteles q pecunia felicitas .
necessaria iudicauit / libros suos absq̄ nūmis
componere potuisset , & aristotelicus iste aristo
telica sine nūmis posset interpretari . Intelli
gis õ q̄ uelit . Oliuerius peripateticus e / ñ
cynicus . At ñ e igitur phīs hec appetere .
Sit ita sane . verū ñ ut phīs e / hec posti
lat / ß ut homo . ytrum ū phīs sit / pecu -
nia petere / postq̄ conuenerus disputabimus . Vale
Salutat te Laurentius bone cultus minime fic /
poeta astronomicus / astronomusq̄ poeticus .:

Neq̄ amor sine religione / neq̄ religio sine amore laudatur.

Marsilius ficinus philippo carronio lucensi . Mitto
ad te amorem quē promiseram . Mitto & religionem .
vt agnoscas / & amorē meū religiosū esse /
& religionē amatoria . Sane ita mea comparata
tū est / ut neq̄ amor honestus sit / in religio
suo / neq̄ religio uera / in amore suscepta .
Salutat te Angelus manettus / Jannoctij oratoris
filius / paterne uirtutis heres .:

THE LETTERS OF MARSILIO FICINO

Volume 3
(Liber IV)

The Letters of
MARSILIO FICINO

Translated from the Latin by members of the Language
Department of the School of Economic Science, London

VOLUME 3
being a translation of
Liber IV

SHEPHEARD-WALWYN

This translation first published 1981 by
Shepheard-Walwyn (Publishers) Ltd
26 Charing Cross Road (Suite 34)
London WC2H 0DH

Reprinted 1994

ISBN 0 85683 045 3

Publisher's Note:

The beehive motif shown on the title page appears on
a number of Ficino manuscripts which were illuminated
for Lorenzo de' Medici's library.
The endpapers show two pages in Ficino's own hand
from a manuscript containing Book I of his *Letters*. This
is now in the Biblioteca Nazionale Centrale, Florence
(Cod. Naz. II IX 2).

British Library Cataloguing in Publication Data

Ficino, Marsilio
  [Epistolae, *English*]. The letters of
  Marsilio Ficino.
  Vol. 3
  1. Ficino, Marsilio
  I. Title   II. The Letters of Marsilio
  Ficino
  195   B785.F4

ISBN 0-85683-045-3

Printed and bound in Great Britain by Alden Press, Oxford

Contents

Acknowledgements

Once again the translators would like to express their gratitude to Professor Paul Oskar Kristeller of Columbia University, New York, who has generously given of his remarkable learning on the Italian Renaissance, assisting especially with the textual sources and the Notes on Correspondents. He has also given invaluable help on Corsi's *Life of Marsilio Ficino*.

An especial word of thanks is due to Professor Nicolai Rubinstein of Westfield College, University of London, who has made many valuable suggestions concerning the translation of the letters and the Notes. Thanks are also due to Professor Margaret King of Brooklyn College, City University of New York, for assistance on the biographical notes about the Venetian humanists, Marco Aurelio and Febo Capella. We should like to acknowledge with gratitude the help of Mr D. L. Stockton of Brasenose College, Oxford, in clarifying the text of Aristotle's inscription to Plato (mentioned by Ficino in his 'Life of Plato') and suggesting a verse translation which we have used.

The translators are pleased to acknowledge the kind cooperation of the Vatican Library, Rome, the Riccardiana, Laurenziana and Nazionale Centrale Libraries, Florence and the Berlin, Staatsbibliothek Preussischer Kulturbesitz, in providing copies of the relevant manuscripts. They are likewise indebted to the Wolfenbüttel, Herzog August Bibliothek who, in addition, have provided the transparency that has been used on the jacket of this book.

Letter Titles

1 Nemo est, cui possit invidere, qui videre possit, quot omnes intus et extra furiis agitamur
No one can be envied, who can see how many times we all are driven both inwardly and outwardly by the Furies

2 Cum rationi et consilio satisfeceris, cunctis satisfecisse putato
When you have satisfied reason and counsel, consider yourself to have satisfied all

3 Frustra sapit, qui non sibi ipse sapit
He who is not wise regarding himself, wastes his wisdom

4 Mundanorum medicina morborum est supermundani dei cultus
The medicine for worldly maladies is adoration of God who is above the world

5 Non quid quisque, sed quo animo det, considerare debemus
We ought to consider, not what someone gives, but the spirit in which he gives

6 Quam turpe est amare pecunias, tam honestum amare hominem, tam etiam necessarium et beatum, amare deum
It is as shameful to love money as it is honourable to love man, and necessary and blessed to love God

7 Qualis in se quisque est, talia cuique sunt quae accipit
As each is in himself, so to each are those things which he receives

8 Mundana omnia discordia componuntur. Omnia discordia et ipsa sibi et aliis opponuntur
By discord are all worldly things held together in place, by discord are all things held in opposition both to themselves and to others

21 Tunc maxime commendas aliquem, cum ostendis illius esse, cui
commendas
*You commend someone most highly when you show him to belong to the one
to whom you make the commendation*

22 Quando divino afflante spiritu amor accenditur, saemper amante altero
redamat alter. Saepe altero cogitante, idem cogitat alter
*Since love is kindled by the breath of a divine spirit, when one loves, the other
always returns love; often when one thinks, the other thinks the same*

23 Quando divino afflante spiritu amor accenditur, saemper amante altero
redamat alter, saepe altero cogitante, idem cogitat alter
*Since love is kindled by the breath of a divine spirit, when one loves, the other
always returns love; often when one thinks, the other thinks the same*

24 Nihil infirmius quam humanus amor, nihil firmius quam divinus amor
*Nothing is less constant than human love, nothing more constant than divine
love*

25 Frustra nimium in rebus his quae sibimet nequaquam sufficiunt, nos-
tram sufficientiam affectamus
*Vainly and to excess we strive for our satisfaction in those things which in no
wise satisfy themselves*

26 Transitus repentinus a minimo lumine ad maximum, atque a maximo
ad minimum, aciem impedit
*A sudden transition from the least light to the greatest, and also from the greatest
to the least, blunts the keen edge of vision*

27 Quod animus immortalis sit. Atque cur cum sit divinus, saepe tamen
vitam agit bestiae similem
*That the soul is immortal. And why, though it be divine, it often leads a life
similar to that of a beast*

28 Solus omnia possidet qui a nullo, praeter deum, penitus possidetur
He alone possesses all things who is inwardly possessed by nothing but God

29 Cum primum fatum impugnare nitimur, expugnamus
As soon as we strive to oppose fate, we overcome it

30 Multos habet servos, qui multis servit
He has many servants, who serves many

Preface

THIS is the third volume of letters translated by the Language Department of the School of Economic Science. It represents the fourth book of Ficino's *Epistolae*, covering mainly the period from 1st March to 1st August, 1477. A number of letters, however, fall outside this period, notably the letters in praise of philosophy (letter 13) and of medicine (letter 14), which were written as speeches, presumably to academic audiences, in Ficino's youth. The last two letters in the volume were written in 1478 and 1479 to Platonists in Hungary. They were originally included in the fifth and sixth books respectively, but were transferred when Books III and IV (volumes 2 and 3 of the present translation) were presented to King Matthias of Hungary.

The period covered by this volume of letters is that leading up to the Pazzi conspiracy against the rule of the Medici. In the conspiracy, which was followed by a war against Florence waged by a powerful alliance of states led by Pope Sixtus IV, Lorenzo de' Medici's brother, Giuliano, was murdered in Florence Cathedral and Lorenzo himself was wounded. Two of Ficino's correspondents, Francesco Salviati and Jacopo Bracciolini, were executed for complicity. Although Ficino would not have known of the plan to murder the Medici, a letter in this volume (letter 36) to Bracciolini seems to indicate that he did know of the conspirators' hostile intentions, and a further one to Pace (letter 8), written less than a fortnight before the attempt, shows that he understood that war would be the inevitable consequence of their disaffection. In Ficino's letters to Salviati and Bracciolini it is clear that he is persistently and strongly discouraging them from taking any rash action.

During the period covered by the letters in this volume Ficino was working on a revision of his translations of Plato's dialogues and his commentaries on them. The whole of Book IV (volume 3) concentrates, even more than the first two volumes, on the philosophy of Plato. Some of the letters consist largely of passages taken from the dialogues. The largest single letter, about a quarter of the volume, is a life of Plato, based mainly on Diogenes Laertius. This life also forms the introduction to Ficino's translation of the dialogues of Plato. It furnishes some interesting parallels with Ficino's own life, as described in the biography by Giovanni Corsi, which is included, partly for this reason, at the end of this volume. Both philosophers led celibate and ascetic lives. Both had close relations with heads of state, whom, to some extent, they influenced by their philosophy. Ficino regarded the life and character of Plato as his model. He wrote in the proem to Book 2 of *De Vita Libri Tres* (*Opera* p. 509), 'Although the spirit of our Plato lives and will live as long as the world itself shall live, yet my spirit always impels me, after worshipping the divine, to observe the life of Plato above all else.' Ficino consciously based his academy on that of Plato, as it is described by the ancient Platonic writers, and devoted his whole life to making the philosophy of Plato a living philosophy to his contemporaries.

A central theme of this volume is the liberation of Man through philosophy. Both the passages which he quotes in full from the dialogues—the analogy of the cave (letter 26) and the many-headed beast (letter 27)—relate to this. Above all, the letter on the nature and education of a philosopher (letter 18) delineates the precise steps by which a man is freed from desire, so that he may attain knowledge of Truth.

Textual Sources

The following are the manuscripts which contain Book IV of the letters, with the sigla of each as given in Kristeller's *Supplementum Ficinianum* I, V–LV:

Name of MS and shelf mark		Sigla	Contains Books	Library
Guelferbytanus	73 Aug. fol.	G1	I–VIII ⎫	Wolfenbüttel,
Guelferbytanus	10 Aug. 4°	G2	III–IV ⎬	Herzog
Guelferbytanus	12 Aug. 4°	G4	III–IV ⎭	August
Riccardianus	797	R10	I–VII	Riccardiana, Florence
Laurentianus	90 Sup 43	L28	I–VIII	Laurenziana, Florence
Berolinensis	Lat. fol. 374	Be	I–VII	Berlin, Staatsbibliothek Preussischer Kulturbesitz

Some individual letters are also contained in the following manuscripts:

Name of MS and shelf mark	Sigla	Contains Letter(s)	Library
Vat. Lat. 5953 Folio 321	V10	18, 19	Vatican
Magl. VIII, 1423	M7	18, 19 ⎫	Nazionale
1441	M9	38 ⎬	Centrale,
Folio 131 r. & v.	S	25, 33 ⎭	Florence

Ficino kept archetypes of his letters, but the archetype for Book IV has been lost. Of the existing manuscripts for Book IV as a whole, G4 and R10 are the most authoritative, particularly since they are in the handwriting of Sebastiano Salvini, Ficino's cousin and secretary. However, the best sources for letters 18 and 19 are M7 and V10. G4 contains only Books III and IV and was Ficino's original dedication copy for King Matthias of Hungary (see letter 1, Vol. 2). It was written in 1481 or 1482. At one point it was reputedly lost and a second copy of Books III and IV was thus subsequently made for King Matthias. This manuscript is G2 and is dated 1484.

Three of the printed editions, Venice 1495, Basle 1576 and Paris 1641 are mentioned in the Notes on the Latin Text and are referred to as V, B and P respectively. The Venice edition is of considerable authority, since it is almost certain that Ficino made amendments to the text immediately prior to publication in 1495. Apart from these three printed editions of the letters there is at least another separate edition of Ficino's *Epistolae* (Nuremburg, 1497, ed. Koberger) and perhaps an undated Prague edition about 1500. There are also some partial editions (see *Supplementum Ficinianum*, I, p. lxvii–lxviii).

Where there are discrepancies in the text, G4 has mainly been followed (except in letters 18 and 19) as generally the most reliable source, but M7, V10, G1, G2, L28, Be, M9 and the Venice edition, have all been consulted. Discrepancies of any importance in the text are set out very fully in the Notes on the Latin Text (except as noted in the prefatory remarks to those Notes, p. 100). In these the comparison is given between the most important manuscripts and the three most important printed editions. However a critical edition is proposed which will take into account all the manuscripts and these three printed editions. This critical edition is intended to be presented in the form of a parallel text and published as soon as opportunity allows.

As regards paragraphs, there are some marked in G4 and R10 in the longer letters. These have mostly been followed and others have been added by the translators where the sense requires.

THE TRANSLATORS

The
Letters

THE FOURTH BOOK[a] OF

THE LETTERS OF

MARSILIO FICINO OF FLORENCE

I

Nemo est, cui possit invidere, qui videre possit, quot[b] omnes
intus et extra furiis agitamur

No one can be envied, who can see how many times we
all are driven both inwardly and outwardly by the Furies[1]

Marsilio Ficino[c] of Florence to Lorenzo Franceschi, the son of
Domenico.

PYTHAGORAS charged his disciples not[d] to eat brain or heart.[2] That
is, they should not consume the brain with empty thoughts, nor
burn out the heart[e] with excessive cares. If all things happen by
chance, they labour in vain who presume to control completely, and
to manage by fixed principles of reasoning, affairs which in countless
ways happen beyond reason. If all things come from[f] fate, those
who strive to avoid what is an unavoidable necessity fall more
heavily into fate, for to it they are adding their own labour. Lastly,
whether our affairs are said to come from chance or fate, divine
providence, by reason, puts unreasonable chance in order, and gently
tempers stern fate in accordance with the good. Thus all things
become ordered and good to those who willingly unite with the
divine will.

For these men alone, what is within the mind accords with external events; but for everyone else, at every point they are at
variance. These men alone make what is necessary voluntary and
what appears evil good.

Just as the pure mind rejoices in universal good, so the impure
mind is afflicted with every evil. Just as the greatest light plunders
and appropriates to itself all other lights, so the greatest evil on
earth, an evil man, draws from all quarters every evil to himself.
He brings much more onto himself than he would receive from
elsewhere. Just as we are insatiable for what is good, so, in some
strange way, are we almost insatiable for evil. Present evils we do
not so much experience as strengthen; past evils we seek again;

future evils we seize in advance; those not in the future we invent. I need not mention the perversity of mind from which we suffer adversities; do we not so misuse prosperity that happiness itself becomes our greatest unhappiness? External success for us[g] is no more than the point of departure from reason and law, and what is soundness of body for us but an unsoundness of mind? Also,[h] beauty and bodily strength often lead to deformity and weakness of soul. Oh, how deformed we are! How often in our deformed state do we set upon that which God makes beautiful. Alas! How ungrateful we are to God, the giver of all good things! How frequently we condemn his works and his governance! The more our stores abound with his good fruits, the more do we produce thorns and weeds within ourselves and sow them at home and abroad. And although we produce and sow bad things, we are nonetheless astonished if we then reap the worst and we blame the stars or God and not our own[i] husbandry. Therefore no one can be envied, who can see how many times we all are driven both inwardly and outwardly by the Furies. In your homeland it would be difficult for you to perceive who is happier than anyone else. Outside it, it would be harder still to see who is most miserable. In both cases the reason is almost the same: in your own country each rejoices with the greatest joy, here each of us is afflicted with the greatest pain. Unless we are completely blind, we should see clearly from this that since our sowing[j] does so badly on earth, it is not earthly but heavenly and, if rightly cultivated, will bear heavenly fruit.

2

Cum rationi et consilio satisfeceris, cunctis satisfecisse putato

When you have satisfied reason and counsel, consider yourself to have satisfied all

Marsilio Ficino to[a] his fellow philosopher.

As I hear, you are much disturbed because those things which you understand yourself to have performed with sure reason, are condemned by many. Do you make of yourself so great a thing, friend, that you would wish those who do not spare God to spare a man?

What can be more beautifully or perfectly executed than those things which come from God, who is the highest reason? Yet in these divine works he is everywhere disparaged. We bristle at spirits, blame the stars, condemn the times, and also find fault with the forms and properties of plants and animals. We carp at men, assiduously bewail our lot. What we have freely received from God displeases us, what we in our ingratitude[b] have done, pleases us so much that we displease God. As often as you are charmed by your new works as by your own new-born child, pray make the effort to yield to reason[c] and submit to counsel. When you have satisfied searching reason and the proven counsel of the wise, consider yourself to have satisfied all men. For thus you have satisfied truth itself, which is greater than all. But, if what you have thought, spoken and done in accord with such reason is condemned in other places, bear in mind that a sign of good food is that it displeases bad taste, but proof of bad food is that it pleases bad taste.

Farewell, and once your will has submitted to true reason, be not disturbed if what follows is beyond your will.

3

Frustra sapit, qui non sibi ipse sapit

He who is not wise regarding himself, wastes his wisdom[1]

Marsilio Ficino to the moral philosopher without morals: greetings.

How absurd is a tailor whose clothes are all torn!
  How useless is a doctor who is always sick!
  How distressing a musician whose lyre is untuned to his voice!
  Just as base is a moral philosopher without morals.
  He who speaks well but acts badly, speaks in vain, whether he is preaching good to men who will not believe him, or beseeching gifts from the gods who will not grant them.

4

Mundanorum medicina morborum[a] est supermundani dei cultus

The medicine for worldly maladies is adoration of God who is above the world[1]

Marsilio Ficino to Bernardo Bembo of Venice, the illustrious knight.

SINCE man's heavenly Father has ordained that our homeland will be heaven, we can never be content while we dwell on earth, a region far removed from our homeland. Yet such a fate is common, not only to men, but to all created things without exception, so that nowhere do they seek rest save at their own source; and for the sake of rest they try to set their end where they had their beginning. Thus water and earth descend to the depths;[b] fire and air seek the heights; moles and suchlike hide themselves in the bowels of the earth; most other creatures tread the surface of the earth; fish born in the sea, swim in the sea. Even so the souls of men, by a common, natural impulse, continually seek heaven, whence they are created, and the King of heaven, beyond. But since the natural desire for God, instilled in us by God, ought not to be unfulfilled (otherwise supreme reason, which does nothing in vain, has bestowed it upon us in vain), it follows that the souls of men are eternal, in order that one day they may be able to reach the eternal, divine good which their nature desires.

From what we have said it follows that, as our souls are never fulfilled with earthly food, nor while they gorge on earthly things can they enjoy the heavenly feast, so in this life they strive with all their might to cling to the King of heaven. For the less they are tainted by the bitter tastes of earth, and the more they are refreshed by the sweet waters of heaven, the more eagerly are they drawn towards the spring of sweetness which is above heaven. The nearer we approach the Lord of the world, the further we depart from worldly slavery. And, as in our homeland we hold fast to Him by beholding and rejoicing, so, away from that homeland, we hold fast to Him by total loving and adoring.[c]

For this reason, nowhere is there found a medicine adequate for earthly diseases, except divine love and worship. Nor is that wrong. For in any illness, where the medicine does not overcome the condition of the evil humour, it is transformed into the humour, disorders the body, saps the strength and thus increases the burden upon them. Therefore, as all our infirmity and adversity is of the body, and worldly, undoubtedly anyone who tries to help an ill of this sort with bodily and worldly medicines labours in vain. Believe me, the need here is for a far stronger medicine; a medicine, I say, which is spiritual and above the world, whence it may drive out bodily and worldly illnesses.

Were we suffering only from one ailment or another, then perhaps any doctor would suffice. But our plague is everything evil. Therefore our antidote[2] is everything good. Our disease is insatiable desire and continual turbulence, therefore our doctor is immeasurable good and eternal peace. Should anyone deny that our medicine is the true adoration of God, there is no remedy left for his ills, and all hope of health is removed.

But in truth, he who trusts in divine remedies, grows strong as soon as he trusts.

5

Non quid quisque, sed quo animo det, considerare debemus

We ought to consider, not what someone gives, but the spirit in which he gives[1]

Marsilio Ficino and Giovanni Cavalcanti[a] to Giorgio Antonio Vespucci, an excellent and most learned citizen: greetings.

I AM giving you our book on true piety,[2] not that I may instruct in piety a man who is already distinguished by his piety, but because I consider that by this one offering, more than by all my discourses, I shall satisfy piety itself; I deem I shall also satisfy my pious friend who,[b] since he always glows with pious love, measures the love itself in every thing rather than its result. For he knows that in reality there is nothing great in the outward circumstances; conversely, there is nothing in great love that is not great. Furthermore, he knows that nothing great is ever given by one who has never wished to give anything more than the thing he has given. On the other hand, he knows that nothing small is given by one who considers that in comparison with his desire to give a greater, whatever he gives is small. Lastly, he knows that one should look not to the hand but to the heart of the giver, and as much as the one wishes to bestow, so much the other is said to owe. For, even if not immediately in hand, nevertheless the gift is received by us in the heart, as soon as we know what the friend wished to give.

He who can give new things daily, never gives anything excellent; he alone bestows the most excellent things for whom there is nothing left to give a second time since, at one and the same time, he bestowed himself, and with himself all that was his. So, to put the matter briefly, either we give nothing or everything. He who gives us some thing, but not his heart, is not offering a gift; he is either leaving something on deposit, or bribing us, or perhaps ensnaring us. But he instantly bestows everything who gives the self which possesses everything.

Farewell.

6

Quam turpe est amare pecunias, tam honestum amare hominem, tam etiam necessarium et beatum, amare deum

It is as shameful to love money as it is honourable to love man, and necessary and blessed to love God

Marsilio Ficino to Piero Guicciardini, distinguished both by his writing and his conduct: greetings.

THERE is as much shame in loving money as there is honour in loving a man worthy of love. No one doubts, provided he has ever loved anything at all, that the lover takes himself from himself and gives himself to the beloved. Money, on the contrary, can take possession of the man who loves it but can give nothing back. Hence such a lover possesses neither money nor himself. However, he who loves a man who returns his love, in so far as in loving he gives himself to the other, so far does he receive himself whilst being loved in return. Indeed, to speak more precisely, he receives double measure, for this reason: he who has given one soul receives two. Further, just as it is clearly honourable and profitable to care for a man worthy of friendship, so it is necessary and blessed to love God, the first source of love and beauty, without whose fire no one is able to love anything, without whose splendour nothing can be loved. Farewell, fortunate one, and commend me to that illustrious citizen, your father Jacopo.

1st March, 1476.
Florence.

7

Qualis in se quisque[a] est, talia cuique sunt quae accipit

As each is in himself, so to each are those things which he receives

Marsilio Ficino to Giovanni Aurelio of Rimini and Giovanni Pietro Cortusi of Padua, his fellow philosophers: greetings.

IT is not evil to fall into those things which are commonly called evil, unless you deserve evil. For one does not suffer evil unless one is evil. It is no good to have those things which are called good unless you deserve good. For one does not enjoy good things unless one is good. The internal does not depend on the external, rather does the external depend on the internal. As each is in himself, so to each is that which he receives. It is not chance we are allowed to bewail so much as choice. We are continually pursuing evil thoughts; evils assail us from every quarter. Daily we chase after evils: deservedly evils chase us. We exercise utmost cruelty, in turn cruelty exercises us. We flee from mercy and mercy flies from us. The more wilfully we flee from human justice, the more does divine justice overtake us, whether we will or no.[b] In the very crime is the punishment of the crime, the reward of good is in the good. We do good only tomorrow, so only tomorrow receive the good. Today, we do evil, and we suffer evil today. We are all in discord with ourselves; in turn all things are discordant to us. If you rightly temper the movements of the mind, as the Persian Magi teach, you will then temper all things to yourself: the bodily humours, seasons of the year, plants, all living beings and heaven. Indeed, without any doubt, you will temper them if you set the mind in order with as much care as architects order stones, painters colour and line,[c] musicians voices, and poets words. And, I may say in conclusion, nothing in you will appear out of order, if you set the brain in order, as you would your hair which covers the brain.

Farewell and, lest you attend to other things in vain, first of all attend to yourself.

8

Mundana omnia discordia componuntur. Omnia discordia et
ipsa sibi et aliis opponuntur

*By discord are all worldly things held together in place,
by discord are all things held in opposition both to
themselves and to others*

Marsilio Ficino desires peace for his Pace[1] but fears war.

YOU wrote to me recently, my Pace, as is your custom, a very kind
and elegant letter; but I wrote nothing to you because I considered
that nowhere was there peace, since I regarded all things to be
inwardly filled with discord. But now I have just found my Pace[2]
where I have long been finding my peace. Jove, as they who understand heavenly things declare, is the author of human peace.
Rinaldo Orsini, child of Jove, nourishes[a] both my Pace and my
peace. As you request, I will earnestly commend you to the child
of Phoebus.[3] But I beseech you, in your turn commend me to the
child of Jove. However, before bringing this letter to a close, unless
perhaps you think it absurd, after peace, I want to philosophise with
you a little about war.

The evil spirits are in opposition to the blessed angels, the signs
of the Zodiac to each other, planets to planets, elements to elements,
plants to plants, animals to animals. Furthermore movement is set
against stillness, deprivation against possession, light against darkness, the white and clear against the black, sound against silence,
high notes against low ones, the fragrant[b] against the fetid, the salty
against the insipid; and, as the Aristotelians[4] believe, sharp and bitter
against sweet, hot against cold, dry against wet, light against heavy,
dense against fine, rough against smooth, and finally, hard against
soft.

Fortune and fate are opposed to the body, the bodily humours to
one another, limbs to limbs, the body itself to the soul, the senses
to reason, one emotion to another, vice is set against virtue and the
vices against each other, opinion is opposed to opinion and finally,
desire to desire.

Of all things, the virtues alone, if they are found anywhere, so accord that the man who pursues but one of them acquires them all. Other things, however, nowhere more accord than in their very discord. Who should therefore wonder that mankind is driven by its own unceasing discord. By discord all things are held together in place. By discord all things are held in opposition both to themselves and to others.

All things sound in consonance outwardly only where inwardly nothing is in dissonance; furthermore nothing is inwardly dissonant where either pure truth holds sway, or the splendour of pure truth shines forth in abundance, or the heat of that same splendour glows. First is God, second is the contemplation of God, third is the love and adoration of God. These things[c] are able to give us that peace, my Pace, which the world, being everywhere full of discord, cannot give. But, lest perhaps by reasoning any more about war, I should seem by this lengthy discourse to have declared war on your eyes and ears, I will say farewell.

13th April, 1478.[5] [d]

9

Ut sortem in melius mutes, animae figuram in melius muta[a]

In order to change your lot for the better, change the form of your soul for the better[1]

Marsilio Ficino greets Mankind.

TODAY, while I was inquiring within myself for the main reason why men constantly lead[b] so laborious a life on earth, there came to mind a game in which people walk along on the palms of their hands and the crown of their head, with their legs in the air. Furthermore, they endeavour with one eye to survey everything on earth and with the other everything in the heavens. Then whatever presents itself on the ground they attempt to grasp with nostrils, lips and fingers. Conversely, whatever hangs above them they attempt to handle and gather in with their feet, and whatever they touch[c] they undertake to carry. Disgraceful sight; wretched monstrosity! These are not men, nor are they animals. They appear to me like those Stygian trees, among whose bitter leaves no fruit is to be found.[2] Could anything more monstrous be imagined, anything more laborious, or more onerous? Such, O[d] my friends, are we ourselves, almost all of us. Alas, wretched ones, almost all of us foolishly subject the head of the soul, that is reason,[e] to the senses, which are the soul's feet. Then, with the mind thus abased to the level of earth, we trust that we may gain knowledge of things celestial as well as earthly. With the feet of the soul, the very lowest part, we try in vain to attain the very highest parts of nature. And while we struggle to make use of everything for ourselves we carry around the burden of everything. Alas, what insane misery we labour under all this time, what miserable insanity! Why do we bewail our lot or fortune? Why do we scheme audaciously to change fortune? To alter the course of fate? O soul, I pray you, change this game, set your form aright! For thus shall you change fortune and alter the course of fate, and in an instant change for the better the form of the world itself for you.

10

Pura neque impure quaeras, neque postquam inveneris
impuris communia facias

*You may neither seek pure things in an impure way nor,
after you have found them, may you reveal them to
impure men*

Marsilio Ficino to the magnanimous Lorenzo de'Medici: greetings.

WHEN, on the Kalends of November last, I had composed one letter
to Giovanni Cavalcanti on the rapture of Paul into[a] the third heaven
and another to Febo Capella on the celestial and supercelestial
light,[1][b] I soon afterwards unhappily contracted that disease of the
eyes to which doctors give the name cataract[2] and which, they
affirm, betokens the onset of blindness. Although I have tried prac-
tically everything that is employed by doctors who are the heirs of
Apollo, the shining father of doctors, Apollo himself, has not yet
restored to me the light I once had.

Alas! How different is the nature of all other things from that of
light, my Lorenzo! Those who shun noises, smells or tastes, certainly
escape such things; and those who particularly search for things of
this kind are chiefly the ones who obtain them. But, alas, he who[c]
with all his strength seeks out light itself, is apt to lose it, as much
as he who seeks to flee far away from it. Paul of Tarsus, whilst
fleeing with precipitate steps from the true sun and pursuing the
light of the very same sun with impious arms, was deprived of all
light, as it is recorded.[3] Marsilio, on the other hand, whilst seeking
to serve the sun and tend its light, has also nearly been deprived of
it. Hence, yesterday, while the moon was in conjunction with the
sun, a prayer to the divine sun came to me. Perhaps the prayer is
somewhat obscure, but in time it will become clearer, I hope, when
my human sun has illumined this[d] moon of mine (and his) at least
once with the rays[e] of his eyes. Farewell.

O, Sun! purging all men's hearts with your flames, do you wish
so very much to be inaccessible to any mortal when, in fact, you
are of all things most accessible to everyone? O, Sun! Source of

Justice! Sun! Model of generosity! As urgently as you incite me to
seek you out, so shine back on me; with just such brilliance, with
just such healing. Have I, perhaps, dared to raise eyes that are too
impure to the purest light? In this event, I confess, I have perhaps
been Phaeton.[4] Nevertheless, Phoebus, I have been and I am, yours,
so cleanse me with your heat, I pray, and cherish me. As you can
cast your rays through everything, Phoebus, so can you heal everything with your health-giving flames; for, unlike Julian, the Platonist[5] and former, but apostate Christian, I have not, being sunless,
yet hymned the very sun himself. Nor, in company with Claudian,[6]
have I impiously sung of your dear[f] sister, Proserpine, snatched, as
the story goes, into the underworld. But rather, with Luke, Hierotheus and Dionysius,[7] I have honoured your son, a certain Aesculapius, that doctor of souls from Tarsus,[8] who was carried off into
the world above. And I have not, like Stesichorus and Homer,
depicted the ill-fated seizure of Helen,[9] that is earthly appearance,
but, as is the way of true Platonists, I have depicted[g] the sublime
upward soaring of the heavenly mind. Nor have I, like[h] Numenius,[10]
indiscriminately made public the Eleusinian mysteries; nor, like
Pherecydes of Syros,[11] disclosed to any earthly man the secrets[i] of
heavenly beings; nor, like Hipparchus the Pythagorean,[12] have I ever
made common to everyone the Delphic mysteries of the sacred Seer,
which are proper to very few. Nor, as was the way with Dionysius
of Syracuse,[13] have I attempted to lay before the impure senses of
the crowd the Apollonian[14] sense of Plato. I have not spoken openly
of that about which men are not permitted to speak; I have not
given what is holy to dogs or pigs[15] for it to be torn into shreds. On
the other hand, it certainly seems to me that I have revealed to men
like Oedipus[j] as many secret things as I myself have seen; however,
to all the ignorant[16] I have given them completely veiled.

What now, Phoebus? What do you most want me to do? You
will send me, I suppose, to Ananias[17] at Damascus, whither you
once sent the blind Saul, where he immediately regained his lost
sight. However, I wish that Ananias for me, Phoebus, might be that
child of yours, victorious Medici, once born in your morning rays.[18]
I have just set out for Damascus, my guide for the journey being
that very son of the Platonic sun. To him who is indeed your child,
but my Ananias, I have made a little offering in pledge of a greater
sacrifice, the remainder of which I will shortly give him.

Therefore Phoebus, now give back to me, if it is your will, give back to me I beseech you, the light I have long desired.

14th April, 1477.

II

Honestum agendum est, quia placeat, placere debet, ut deo placeat

A good action should be performed because it is pleasing. It ought to please so that it may please[a] God

Marsilio Ficino to Lotterio Neroni: greetings.

GREAT as was my satisfaction with all I said and wrote at the beginning of my studies, Lotterio, thereafter my daily dissatisfaction with all my work has been nearly as great. Yet every day I am impelled, I know not by what fate or spirit, to write something, even against my will. So in order to offend Marsilio and others as little as possible, it is always foremost in my mind, when writing, to be as brief as I can. But, by being too brief in my eagerness to avoid a tedious prolixity, I sometimes in a way do not make myself clear. Certainly I often perplex others. But this usually happens, and rightly, to those who have not learned to maintain measure in things.

Now look! How ridiculous it will seem, O friend, how absurd that I should be compelled to explain an intimate[b] letter to my friend, who sometimes appears to be like a second Mercury in his power of comprehension. But I think I am really under no such compulsion, for while you seek from us clearer and simpler instruc-

tion, you give us abundant instruction. You have failed to disguise
your subtlety, O pseudo-ignoramus! For I have seen what makes
you ask for a clearer explanation of my letter. It is a burning desire
for further discourse with me, not zeal for plainer instruction. Thus,
cunning fellow, you now demand not elucidation but loving prolixity. Nonetheless, to satisfy you with a longer discourse, and to use
plainer words for anyone else who perhaps may really require an
explanation, the essence of my previous letter is this:

With every power I have I always endeavour to set in motion
whatever the counsel of the wise, and[c] careful reasoning, persuade
me is good. I am not relating this good to some external benefit,
which would be in the future, short-lived, and dependent on the
choice of men or fortune; but first and foremost to that true joy
which is experienced in the very action of the good. Even if this
good and this joy can be described as temporal, since the good is
not followed, nor the joy experienced continuously in the same
way, yet they lie deep within[d] ourselves and in our will. Indeed,
good of this kind gives satisfaction both in the present and in eternity. I say this not because I now enjoy eternity directly but for no
reason other than that I understand that this good accords with the
form of the good, that is with the eternal knowledge and art of
almighty God. Therefore, just as I have related that good back to
inner joy, so I relate joy back to the form of the good; so that clearly
by this reasoning the good may please[e] me, and thence I myself may
best please God, the good of all good, without whom nothing can
please me.

You say, 'I do not possess happiness at present, but I hope for it
in the future.' Desire happiness, Lotterio, and you will be happy
with present, that is, eternal happiness rather than future happiness.
For if any future happiness is in you, it is happiness for this reason:
that it is contained within that happiness which neither past nor
future touches.

Farewell.

15th April, 1477.

12

Nihil vel[a] mirabilius vel amabilius est quam doctrina probitati coniuncta

There is nothing more wonderful nor more lovely than learning united with virtue

Marsilio Ficino of Florence to Marco Aurelio, the distinguished orator: greetings.

WHEN singular[b] learning, Marco Aurelio, is united with surpassing virtue, from this conjunction, as if of the Sun and Jupiter, such splendour bursts forth from the learning and such fire from the virtue that, by these rays and flames which spread from the rising to the setting sun, the minds of even the most distant peoples are aroused and kindled, gently enticed and violently seized. Thus, on this principle, Marco Aurelio used to entice his youthful Marsilio Ficino, and now seizes him at a ripe age. Now see all this plunder hastening towards you, Marco, as your own: your Marsilio, equally in youth as well as in years. Accordingly, he presents[c] you with six short speeches,[1] the first two of which, in praise of philosophy and in praise of medicine, date from his tender age; the four subsequent ones, concerning the principal practices of the human race, were born this spring. Thus, at long last, they will have been born fruitfully if, in your presence, they are continuously nurtured.

13

Marsilii Ficini oratio de laudibus philosophiae

A speech of Marsilio Ficino in praise of philosophy[1]

MOST noble gentlemen, at this moment my mind is pulled in contrary directions, as has often happened to those[a] about to give an

address on serious subjects. For the ancient custom of this venerable
school and the weighty authority of its founders, both of which
rightly have the strongest possible influence upon me, urge me to
speak today in praise of philosophy.

But when I inwardly consider the power and nature of this subject,
it appears to me to be so noble and excellent that I despair[b] of its
being understood by the human mind or expounded by the human
tongue. The loftiness of the subject, the lowliness of my talent, and
furthermore your awesome aspect, all now make me frightened to
speak. So I falter between silence and speech. Yet, noble gentlemen,
as far as I am able, I shall speak, having concluded that it is preferable
for the subject of my speech not to appear to Marsilio than for
Marsilio not to appear at the behest of his superiors. So you will
forgive me if I fail utterly to express any outstanding[c] praises of
philosophy in accordance with her worth; and everything I say you
will ascribe directly to the divine light by whose illumination we
perceive, by whose rays we understand, and by whose splendour
we reveal everything.[d]

Most excellent gentlemen, the age-old view of the theologians,
confirmed by the reasonings of many philosophers, by which we
have been well taught and in which we have been raised, is this: the
more perfect and worthy of honour each being appears in the natural
order, the closer it approaches the perfection and worth of the first
cause of all, and the more nearly[e] and clearly it represents the image
of this cause within itself. The ancient theology of the Egyptians
and Arabs handed down this: God is the source of being, knowing
and acting.[2] Whence Pythagoras, Heraclitus and Plato, conveying
that theology into Greece, declared that the beginning of creation,
the truth of the teaching and the joy of life are from this selfsame
God. To this Plato bears witness in *The Republic*, *Parmenides* and
Timaeus,[3] as do Iamblichus and Proclus in their theologies.[4]

Following those ancient writers, Dionysius the Areopagite,[5] initially a Platonist and then a Christian, gave very extensive expression in his books to the same view, which was also held much later
by St. Hilary[6] and St. Augustine, the principal Latin theologians.
And so Augustine,[7] in his books on *The True Religion* and *The City
of God*, calls God Himself 'The Maker of All Things', 'The Illuminator of Truth', and 'The Bestower of Happiness'; and he confirms
that this had been systematically treated, albeit in different words,

by the Platonic philosophers many centuries previously. Further-more, that in these three titles of God, first introduced by the ancient philosophers, the Christian Trinity is also comprehended in some way; and lastly, that the three aspects of philosophy[8] discovered and disseminated by Plato correspond to this trinity of ours[f] in all its particulars.

Let that branch of philosophic discourse which sets forth[g] the causes and development of things correspond to God, their source. Let the next branch, in which the origin and method of setting things in order are treated, correspond to God, the illuminator of truth. Let the last part of philosophy, by whose precepts and on whose foundations we lead our lives and direct ourselves, the family and the state in the pursuit of happiness, also[h] be compared in some measure to God, the bestower of happiness.

From this it can now be quite clear that philosophy in every part accords, as I have said, with the Godhead whole and perfect, and contains, so far as it is revealed to us, a full and complete image of the power, wisdom, and goodness of Father, Son and Spirit. Thus it is, that of all the faculties of men none appears closer or more similar to the Godhead than philosophy, and so nothing available to us, save God Himself, is seen as more perfect or more excellent. For which reason Hermes, wisest of the Egyptians, seems, through godlike power, to have explained this, when he declared that men become gods through the light of philosophy.[9] Pythagoras also sounded the same note in the *Golden Verses*;[10] and Plato, in his books on *The Republic*, appointed for philosophers at their death the sacred rites and mysteries that are accorded to the gods.[11] Again, Empe-docles of Agrigentum said that philosophy is a gift of the gods which brings anyone it has touched to such a state that from a lofty mind he holds in contempt everything which is set in motion; from the innermost point of the mind he is illumined by divine rays, and awaits future blessedness with steadfast purpose.[12]

But what is nobler than the declaration made by Aristotle? Whereas the other arts and sciences, aghast at the size and difficulty of the matter, have moved a long way from the search for truth, philosophy alone has never shirked laborious work; she has con-sidered that she is not unworthy of the richest treasures, and that knowledge of these befits her and is of the same birth. And since it is impossible to approach the heavenly regions through bodily strength, the soul, having acquired the power of mental discernment as guide by the gift of philosophy, transcends the nature of all things through contemplation. So said Aristotle.[13]

Finally, to be brief, since she is a gift from heaven, philosophy drives earthly vices far away; firmly subdues fortune; marvellously softens fate; uses mortal gifts most rightly;[i] and bestows immortal gifts according to desire. O treasure, of all things most precious, in no way produced from the bowels of Earth and Pluto, but descending from the topmost point of heaven and from the head of Jove! Without possession of this treasure we cannot make right use of other treasures nor possess anything fruitfully. O surest guide for human life who, firstly, with club of Hercules, puts the monsters of vice to headlong flight! Then, with the shield and spear of Pallas she averts or overcomes the perils of fortune. Lastly, supporting men's souls with the shoulders of Atlas, she frees them from this earthly exile and restores them to their celestial homeland in the fullness of truth and happiness. May what Plato said be justified: that there was once a golden age when wisdom reigned, and that if ever philosophy reigns again the golden age will return.[14] But what are we doing, noble gentlemen? Why do we vainly seek to measure eternity in, so to speak, a moment of time? Not merely a day, but very many years, would be insufficient, were we directly to undertake to adorn blessed philosophy with all her praises.

So there remains nothing more to be said or done, but having left behind all that is set in motion, all that is lifeless, in which there is nothing to be found beyond shadows and phantoms, we should devote ourselves with whole mind and ardent spirit to the study of this divine gift.

For, lower than the human race, those who have no part in philosophy degenerate rapidly, as it were, into beasts. Those, however, who give moderate service to philosophy will without doubt go forth as men fit to teach the learned and rule the rulers. Yet he who, throughout an entire life, devotes himself wholly to her alone, once the body has been laid aside, as it were, will go straight and free to the upper regions and will ascend beyond human form, having become a God of life-giving heaven.[15]

14

Marsilii Ficini oratio de laudibus medicinae

A speech of Marsilio Ficino in praise of medicine[1]

THE Pythagorean and Platonic philosophers who emanated from the fount of philosophy, Hermes Trismegistus, consider that nothing can be examined nor discovered in any way by the mind of men without that principle from which proceed both the mind itself and those things which must be learnt.[a] Hence they believed that the light for contemplating everything is that selfsame God from whom all things originate.[b] For just as the brilliance in the eyes discerns the brilliance of colour within the sun's very light, creator of both colour and eye, so the truthful mind comprehends the truth of any thing within the highest truth,[c] the begetter of every truth and of every mind.

Thus today, led by an ancient custom and the command of our fathers, we are going to speak in praise of medicine, which is said to be descended from Apollo. Turning the sharp point of the mind away from the darkness towards the light—let us therefore humbly invoke the rays of the true and supreme Apollo, so that, cleansed by his wholesome warmth, we may set forth the praise of this cleansing and bring it to perfection, either through his own worth, or at least through our own native powers.

Most distinguished gentlemen, there are three principles by which philosophers have traditionally judged the perfection of any science: the end, the source, and the substance.[2] Now, whether you follow the Hebrew and Arab theologians, or the Greek and Egyptian, the beginnings of medicine emanated from the Godhead itself. For the Hebrews and Arabs claim that Adam, the first father of the human race, acquired that wisdom by divine light. The others, however, maintained that Apollo took that wisdom upon himself from Jove, father of men and of gods, for the welfare of the human race; Apollo then revealed this same wisdom to Aesculapius, from whom sprang those outstanding doctors, Podalirius and Machaon.[3] Many generations afterwards, Hippocrates of Cos brought forth into the light things which, enveloped in obscure parables, had been handed down

by the ancients.[4] And all these whom I have so far mentioned are
said to have been accorded a place in the company of the gods by
every pagan religion.

What should I say of Pythagoras, Empedocles, Democritus, Diocles of Carystus[d], Erasistratus, Praxagoras, Chrysippus, Herophilus,
Serapion, Apollonius, Glacias, Heraclides, Chemison, Plistonicus,
Galen?[5] And of the most eminent and outstanding of Greek philosophers, Plato and Aristotle? We know for certain that all of these
stood out as philosophers of deep penetration and published a large
number of books on the art of healing. And what of the Egyptians,
most ancient of all races, whose priests, without exception, were
outstanding physicians, as Homer,[6] Euripides and Plato[7] attest? What
of the Persian Magi, or priests—Zoroaster, Hostanes,[e] Abstrosicon,
Gobrias, Paxatam, Sinicariondas, Damigeron, Hismoses, Ioannes,
Apollonius, Dardanus—[8] through whom countless books on this art
are said to have been brought to light, which safeguard our health
by reference to movements of the stars, to words, herbs, precious
stones and vapours? And did not Mithridates too, that king of
Pontus to whom twenty-two[f] tongues were intelligible, bestow long
hours of work on studies of this discipline?[9] Also Sabor,[g] King of
the Medes, the divine Avicenna,[10] and many other Arabs, devoted
themselves to this wisdom with fervent endeavour. So did Serapion
and his son Ioannes, besides Ioannes Mesue, Abumeron, Avenzoar,
Rhazes, Averroes, Abugasis, Isaac, Haly, and many other wise
Hebrews and outstanding Arabs.[11]

I need hardly mention the Latin writers, of whom Cornelius
Celsus, Apuleius, Quintus Serenus, Columella, Pliny and Lactantius[12] were the first to compose books in both prose and verse on
the care of health. Those who have followed them are found to be
almost without number and are so well known to you that they
need no further elaboration whatsoever.

Surely it is impossible to discover a source of any branch of
learning more excellent than the birth of medicine; or one which is
equal or even comparable to it. For it proceeds from a god, from
heroes, kings, leaders, Magi, philosophers, and indeed from the
most ancient and wise of all men.

Truly, the substance which is subject to this art, and about which
it turns—whose[h] principles and properties it earnestly seeks—is
Man, upon whom Hermes Trismegistus placed such high value that

he declared Man, after Almighty God, to be virtually the greatest of the Gods.[13] Also, according to the Stoics and the Peripatetics, everything which moves beneath the moon's sphere is created and set in motion for Man's sake. Moreover the Hebrews,[14] Arabs and Christian theologians saw that even the cosmos itself has been established for the sake of Man.

Who cannot see from this that Man, with whom this skill of ours is concerned, is well-nigh the most excellent of all things flowing from God? And hence that the science of caring for Man must be judged the most perfect? Nor would any physician say that his art centres upon Man's body alone, since Phoebus, as[i] may be read in the *Letters of Hippocrates*,[15] considered the care of the soul and of the body to come together in one.

Thus, among the Egyptians and the Persians the same men were both priests and doctors. Plato writes in *Charmides*[16] that those Magi who were physicians of both soul and body, followers of Zamolxis and Zoroaster, believed that everything belonging to the body, good or bad, flows from the soul into the body itself, just as the nature of the eyes flows from the brain, and the nature of the brain from the whole body. Just as it is impossible to heal the eyes unless the brain is healed, and to heal the brain without healing the whole body, so the whole body cannot be strong unless the soul is strong. The health of the soul is in fact cared for by certain invocations to Apollo, that is, by philosophical[j] principles. Furthermore, Socrates said it was common knowledge among the Thracians that it was customary for doctors, by administering some such treatment, to preserve a few men from death.[17] So great is the dominion of the soul over the body, so great its power. The belief in this magic appears to accord with the Hebrew and Christian view that through the initially healthy soul of Adam, the first father, all things were healthy; but that through its subsequent infirmity, all things became infirm.[18] Cornelius Celsus, too, held that the entire and perfect art of medicine was understood when one had the power to look after a man's health by comprehending the movements of his mind and body.[19] In these two both natural and moral contemplation and their application are encompassed.

Avicenna consequently judged the quality of the body to exert the greatest possible influence over the mind for better or worse; and also the dispositions, movements and images of the mind itself to exert the greatest influence over the health, good or bad, of the body.

Has anyone not yet perceived the aim of doctors? It is this: that by their care and dedication life and, moreover, a good life may be sustained. Could anything better or more desirable be added to this? What is closer to or more consonant with Nature than to watch over and preserve what she herself has borne? Illustrious gentlemen, every one of you is aware that human prosperity lies not in the possession of things, but in their enjoyable use. Yet all of sound mind realize that without health, we cannot enjoy the use of anything. Thus, in a hymn to health, Orpheus sang: σου γαρ ἀτερ παντεσιν 'ανωφελη 'ανωοισιν[20], that is 'Without thee, all things are useless to men.' Medicine, therefore, since it either safeguards or restores health, is seen to preserve and re-establish the whole good at the same time. For this reason the sacred writings of the Hebrews rightly instruct us to honour doctors, and Homer truly says: 'One man of medicine is equal in worth to many other men.'[21]

So, my friends, I strongly urge you all, in no way to stint time, money, or labour, so that you may embrace with all your might this most wholesome art, the preserver of human life. Thus you will each be able to watch over the life and prosperity of yourself, then of your family, and finally of everyone else, and to support the other liberal arts, which cannot be learned and practised without health. And ultimately you may prescribe for the good of all peoples, nay even the mightiest kings, all of whom surrender themselves into your hands.[22k]

15

In singulis expertum consule

In everything consult the man of experience

Marsilio Ficino to Lorenzo Buonincontri, the astronomer[a] and poet:
greetings.

WHEN lately I sought a friend, one out of many, whom I might best
consult on whether I had reasoned truly in my treatise on the rapture
of Paul into the third heaven, Lorenzo Buonincontri, the astronomic
poet, and the poetic astronomer, came foremost into my thoughts.
As an astronomer, his own Atlas[1] has long raised him into heaven
on his lofty shoulders. As a poet, his father, Phoebus himself, has
sung with rounded tones on heavenly things. Therefore I shall consider I have portrayed a true image of the divine only when my
Lorenzo has thoroughly approved, for with Atlas as his guide and
Apollo to show him, he has seen the face of the divine.

16

Praestat malam valetudinem bene ferre quam male bonam

It is better to bear a bad state of health well than good
health badly

Marsilio Ficino to his friends: greetings.

WHY, friends, do you so frequently ask whether I am well? Rather
ask whether I have at last recovered. Though others seem born for
good health, I, on the contrary, seem born just for this: to be subject
to continuous ill health. For from the beginning, by a certain weakness of constitution, it has been my lot never to experience for a
whole day full bodily health.

But I weigh the damages of ill-willed Nature[a] against a most
abundant gift of God, so that just as some men bear[b] their good
health badly, I for the most part bear bad health well. Therefore just

as some men[c] are indebted to Nature for a fortunate possession, so am I as greatly indebted to God[d] for its use.

When God Himself is our strength,[1] we cannot be entirely weak.[e] For then strength of spirit is achieved by infirmity of body. Indeed, it is good for me to cleave to God; since, as St. Augustine says, if I will not abide in Him, I shall not be able to abide in myself.[2]

Therefore stand firm, O friends, stand firm in God, who is not moved, and you will stay firm. Find your peace in that which is not troubled and in peace you will live.

17

Omnia dedit semel, qui se ipse dedit

He has given everything once and for all, who has given his very self

Marsilio Ficino to Bernardo Bembo, the illustrious Venetian: greetings.

SCARCELY had I given Jacopo Lanfredini a letter for you in which I wished to be assured that you had received all my works—or rather, yours—when your letter, filled with gravity, wit and love, was given to me in return. But what shall I say about such marvellous gratitude? Some, when they have received something freely given by another, afterwards barely give thanks. Our Bembo, however, when he has received what is by right his own, gives thanks, and indeed most copious thanks.

I, my sweetest Bembo,[a] have been unable to give you anything new for a long time now: I gave everything to you once and for all when I gave you Marsilio. And even if a possession of this kind is of little weight—for I am not of a size to fulfil what you deserve—yet it is no light thing that by your fine conduct you have seized and made captive all other men of letters,[b] no less than myself. For you are the desire of all these men. You are the delight of our people.

26th April, 1477.[c]

18

De Platonica philosophi natura, institutione, actione

On the Platonic nature, instruction and function of a philosopher[1]

Marsilio Ficino to Giovanni Francesco Ippoliti, the distinguished Count of Gazzoldo.

A LONG time ago I wrote rather a lengthy letter to Bernardo Bembo of Venice in praise of philosophy,[2] and lately, something also on the same subject to the distinguished orator, Marco Aurelio.[3] What remains, it seems, is for me to write something about the Platonic nature, instruction, and function of a philosopher, so that it may be more clearly revealed how that precious treasure of philosophy may be most easily rediscovered by us; and, once it is found, by what principle it may lawfully be possessed and measured out.

Since philosophy is defined by all men as love of wisdom (the very name introduced by Pythagoras[4] supports this) and wisdom is the contemplation of the divine, then certainly the purpose of philosophy is knowledge of the divine. This our Plato testifies in the seventh book of *The Republic*, where he says that true philosophy is the ascent from the things which flow and rise and fall, to those which truly are, and always remain the same. Therefore philosophy has as many parts and ministering powers as it has steps by which it is climbed from the very lowest level to the highest. These steps are determined partly by the nature and partly by the diligence of men. For, as Plato teaches in the sixth book of *The Republic*, whoever is to become a philosopher[5] should be so endowed by Nature that, in the first place, he is willing and prepared to enter upon all manner of disciplines; thereafter that he is truthful by nature, completely opposed to all falsehood; in the third place that, having scorned all that is subject to corruption,[a] he directs his mind to that which remains always the same. He must be magnanimous and courageous, so that he neither fears death nor longs for empty glory. Over and above this, he should be born with something of an even temperament, and from nature he should receive already under con-

trol those parts[b] of the mind which are usually carried away by the
feelings. For whoever longs for the truth turns his mind to contemplation of the divine and sets little value on the pleasures of the
body. Beyond this, a philosopher should be of liberal mind. And in
fact the prizing of worthless things is opposed to this and completely
counter to the way of a man intending to contemplate the truth of
things. Above this his will chooses justice, since he is utterly devoted
to truth, moderation and liberality.[c] But most of all, it seems that
he needs sharp insight, memory and magnanimity.

What is more, these three gifts of nature, namely sharp insight,
memory and magnanimity, when discipline and a proper education
have been added, produce a man perfect in virtue. But if they are
neglected, they are said by Plato to be the cause of the greatest
crimes.[6] Therefore, this nature must be given man's greatest care,
so that he who is thus shaped by Nature, from his childhood, learns
letters, the elements of all knowledge. And indeed the unordered
mind of this person must be put in order by use of the lyre; the
body must be exercised by gymnastic[d] games, so that, coming into
a good condition itself, it offers service to the studies of philosophy.
Meanwhile the precepts of the best laws[e] should be heard by him
and fixed in his mind. Thus the mind of the young man should be
formed by honest encouragement, so that it is rendered temperate
and peaceful.[f] This moral education, men in fact call Ethics.

In truth, when the mind is freed from the disturbance of desire
by these means of which we have spoken, it will already have begun
to be loosed from the body; then it must be given knowledge of
mathematics,[7] which concerns number, plane figures,[g] and whole
forms, and their manifold movements. Indeed, since numbers and
figures and the principles of movement belong to the faculty of
thought rather than the outer senses, the mind, by the study of
these, is separated not only from the appetites of the body, but from
its senses also, and applies itself to inner reflection. This is indeed to
meditate on death which, Plato writes in *Phaedo*,[8] is the duty of one
practising philosophy. Through this we are restored to the likeness
of God, as is taught in *Phaedrus* and *Theaetetus*.[9]

However, according to the Platonists, in the thorough understanding of these things there is this order:[10] Geometry follows
Arithmetic; Stereometry, Geometry; Astronomy follows this, and
lastly Music follows Astronomy. For numbers are before figures,

plane figures are before whole forms,[h] but bodies are whole before they are set in motion. The order and ratios of sounds follow movement. Therefore let Arithmetic, which concerns number, come first. Let Geometry, which deals with plane figures, follow. Let Stereometry, which considers whole bodies, follow after this. Let the fourth place be held by Astronomy which raises[i] the sight to the movements of whole bodies, that is, the movements of the spheres. Let Music, which investigates the order of sounds born out of motion, be last.

When these have been thoroughly understood, Plato gives dialectic,[11] that is, knowledge of how truth is made manifest. But he means by dialectic not only that logic which teaches the first and most detailed rules of reasoning, but also the profound skill of the mind freed to comprehend the true and pure substance of each thing, first by physical, then by metaphysical principles. Thus the reason for anything can be made known and finally the light of the mind may be perceived beyond the nature of senses and bodies; and the incorporeal forms of things, which we call ideas, may be understood.[j] By means of these, the same one source of all species, the origin and light of minds and souls, the beginning and end of all, which Plato calls the good itself, may be inwardly perceived. The contemplation of this is wisdom, love of which is most correctly defined as philosophy.

In truth, once the mind of a man practising philosophy has contemplated the good itself, and thence[k] judges what things in human affairs are good, what bad, what dishonourable or honourable, harmful or useful, he organizes human affairs as a model of the good itself. He leads them away from evil, directs them to the good, and by this wise governance he manages personal, family and public affairs, and he teaches the laws and principles of good management. From this laws have their beginning.[l]

For this reason in *Timaeus* Plato asserts that philosophy is a gift of God, and nothing more excellent has ever been granted us by God than this.[12] For the good itself, which is God, could bestow nothing better on a man than a complete likeness of its own divinity, as near as possible. Indeed, who would doubt that God is truth unconfined by the body and providing for all? But the philosopher, by moral instruction and that early education of which we have spoken, frees the mind from desire and the sense of the body, attains truth by dialectic, and makes provision for men by teaching them citizenship. Thus it comes about that philosophy is a gift, a likeness, and a most happy imitation of God. If anyone is endowed with philosophy, then out of his[m] likeness to God he will be the same in earth as He who is God in heaven. For a philosopher is the intermediary between God and men; to God he is a man, to men God. Through his truthfulness he is a friend of God, through his freedom he is possessor of himself, through his knowledge of citizenship he is a leader of all other men. Indeed it is said that the golden age once existed because of such a ruler and Plato prophesied that it will return only when power and wisdom come together[n] in the same mind.[13]

According to Plato, the minds of those practising philosophy, having recovered their wings through wisdom and justice, as soon as they have left the body, fly back to the heavenly kingdom. In heaven they perform the same duties as on earth. United with God in truth, they rejoice. United with each other in freedom, they give thanks. They watch over men dutifully, and as interpreters of God and as prophets, what they have set in motion here they complete there. They turn the minds of men towards God. They interpret the secret mysteries of God to human minds. On this account the ancient theologians justly honoured the minds of those practising philosophy as soon as they were released from the body, just as they honoured the thirty thousand divinities of Hesiod[14] as demi-gods, heroes and blessed spirits.

Thus philosophy, to express it in a few words, is the ascent of the mind from the lower regions to the highest, and from darkness[o] to light. Its origin is an impulse of the divine mind; its middle steps are the faculties[p] and the disciplines which we have described; and its end is the possession of the highest good. Finally, its fruit is the right government of men.[q]

I have communicated these matters to our Francesco Berlinghieri, as a philosopher friend. For the same reason you will also communicate them to our Giuliano Burgo.[r]

19

De Vita Platonis

On the life of Plato[1]

Marsilio Ficino to his own Francesco Bandini: greetings.

IN the last few days I have tried to paint the ideal form of a philosopher in Platonic colours. However, if I had brought Plato himself
into our midst, I would assuredly not have pointed to some picture
of that ideal form of a true philosopher, but to the ideal form itself.
Therefore, let us look closely at our Plato, so that[a] we may see
equally philosopher, philosophy and the ideal form itself, at one and
the same time.

Genealogy[b] and birth of Plato[2]

Plato of Athens, the son of Ariston and Perictione (or Potone) traced
his descent on both sides from Neptune. For Solon was descended
from Nereus[c] and Neptune. The brother of Solon, Dropides, had
a son, Critias the elder, from whom Callaeschrus is descended. He
had two sons, Critias the younger, who was one of the thirty rulers
of Athens, and Glaucon,[d] who was the father of Charmides and
Perictione. Perictione married Ariston[e] and gave birth to Plato,
Adeimantus, Glaucon, and a girl, Potone, who married Eurymedon
and gave birth to Speusippus. Plato's father,[f] Ariston, in turn was
descended from Codrus, the son of Melanthus, who again trace their
descent back to Neptune, as does Solon. It is said to have been well
known in Athens that Ariston tried to approach Perictione, as she
was very beautiful, but his attempts were in vain; then he saw
Apollo in a dream and was commanded by him to keep her free
from conjugal intercourse until she had given birth. Both Laertius
and Policrates[3] write of this.

Plato was born either in Athens or on Aegina seven hundred and
fifty-six years after the capture of Troy, three hundred and thirty-
three years after the founding of Rome and four hundred and
twenty-three years before the coming of Christ.[4] In my book *On*

Love I described the position of the planets at Plato's birth, as I heard of them in my youth.[5] But now I shall draw your attention to their position as described by Julius[g] Firmicus,[6] the astronomer, whose opinion on this matter I consider to be more correct. And it is as follows: Mars, Mercury and Venus are in Aquarius, which is in the ascendant. In the second house the Sun is in Pisces; in the fifth the Moon is in Gemini; in the seventh Jupiter is in Leo, and in the ninth Saturn is in Libra.

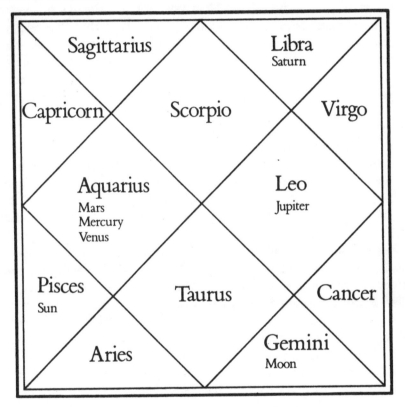

Julius Firmicus claims that such a nativity[h] signifies a man who has the power of wonderful eloquence and approaches all the secrets of the Godhead with divine genius.

The upbringing, natural qualities, learning and even-mindedness of Plato

It is related that while he was in the cradle some bees cast honey onto his infant lips, as a presage of future eloquence.[7]

They say that Socrates in a dream[i] saw on his knee a fledgling cygnet; all at once it grew its feathers and, spreading its wings,[j] flew into the sky, sending forth the sweetest songs. The next day Plato was presented by his father to Socrates who said, 'This is the swan I saw.'[8]

In Plato's youth his poetry came to flower. He composed elegies and two tragedies, which he himself consigned to the flames as soon as he had applied his mind to philosophy.[9] His first learning was imparted to him by the teacher Dionysius; then at the age of twenty he received instruction from Socrates; after the death of Socrates he attached himself to Cratylus, a disciple of Heraclitus, and to Hermogenes,[k] an upholder of the philosophy of Parmenides. When he was twenty-eight he and other disciples of Socrates betook themselves to Euclides at Megara; from here he set out for Cyrene to hear Theodorus the mathematician. Next he went to Italy to the Pythagoreans: Philolaus, Archytas of Tarentum and Eurytus. From them he withdrew to the prophets and priests in Egypt. He had intended to go on to the Magi and the Indians but because of wars in Asia he gave up this plan. Finally he returned to Athens and lived at Academia.[10] It is said (and St. Basil and St. Jerome confirm this)[11] that he chose this unhealthy place in Attica so that the over-fine condition of his body, like the excessive growth of a vine, might be cut back; for he was very strong and handsome. And because of this, his broad shoulders and ample forehead, the outstanding condition of his whole body, and also his richness of speech, he was called Plato, although he had previously been named[l] Aristocles.[12] He was without flaw except perhaps that he had rather a soft voice and some kind of lump just below the neck[m] which marred him a little. Through living at Academia he suffered a quartan fever for eighteen months, but with temperance and care he gained greater strength after his fever than he had had before.

The three military expeditions and sea voyages of Plato[13]

The first voyage. He went on military service three times, first to Tanagra, secondly to Corinth, and thirdly to Delium, where he also gained the prize for valour. He sailed to Sicily three times; the first time to see the island, the marvels of Mount Etna and the craters. He was then in his fortieth year and it was at this time too that

Dionysius, the son of Hermocrates, urged Plato to come and talk with him. Here Plato was discoursing on absolute rule, saying it was not the best because absolute rule would only profit itself alone, unless it were also distinguished by virtue. The story goes that the tyrant, offended and angry, said, 'Yours are the words of idle old men', to which Plato rejoined, 'And yours smack of tyranny.' At these words the enraged tyrant at first actually wanted to kill him, but on the entreaty of Dion and Aristomenes he did not carry this out. However, he did hand him over to Polis of Sparta—who at that time had come to Dionysius as an ambassador—so that Plato might be sold as a slave. Polis took him to Aegina and sold him, whereupon Charmandrus too arraigned him on a capital charge; for, indeed, according to a law passed there it was a capital offence for any Athenian to go to that island. On the other hand, when someone put forward the argument that Plato, thanks to his training, had risen to become a philosopher, and that law spoke of men and not philosophers (who are above men), they acquitted and dismissed him; and they decreed that he should not be killed, but sold. Anniceris[n] the Cyrenian happened to be there, and he redeemed him for twenty *minae* and sent him back to his friends in Athens.

But Polis was defeated by Chabrias and a little later he was drowned in Helice,[14] being told by a spirit, so the story goes, that he was suffering these things on account of the Philosopher. Nor did Dionysius rest; indeed, when he learned[o] what had befallen Polis, he wrote begging Plato not to put a curse on him. Plato wrote back to him that the study of philosophy left him little leisure for thinking about Dionysius. When some other people disparagingly remarked that he had been forsaken by Dionysius, Plato replied, 'On the contrary, Dionysius has been abandoned by Plato.'

The second[P] *voyage.*[15] On the second occasion he went to Dionysius the Younger, having been invited by him and by Dion to expound philosophy. He was also led by the hope that through his counsels he would bring it about that there a republic or kingdom would evolve from a tyranny; and that he would see, somthing he had been ardently desiring for a long.time, namely a most philosophical form of government, in which either the philosophers govern or the rulers study philosophy. For he believed that in no other way could states avoid misery. He wanted all this to be brought about not by force or deceit but, once Dionysius had been won over, by philosophical reasoning. But about four months after Plato's arrival, Dionysius was persuaded, by false accusations of plotting against the tyranny, to banish Dion. Nevertheless he gladly continued to show favour to Plato. But Plato returned to his own country.

The third[q] voyage.[16] On the third occasion Plato came intending to reconcile Dion with Dionysius, after he had been implored again and again[r] by both of them; he was asked by Archytas also. On that occasion Dionysius sent a well-provisioned trireme, Archidemas the Pythagorean orator and many noblemen to meet Plato, and he himself also welcomed him ashore with a chariot drawn by four[s] white horses.[17]

Plato asked for the promised recall of Dion, and in addition for land and men, so that they all might live there in accordance with the constitution of his Republic. Although Dionysius had promised this he drew back[t] from fulfilling it. But when Plato publicly accused Dionysius of having broken faith—first with Plato himself over the reinstatement of Dion, and then with Plato's Theodotus over the protection of Heraclides—he had Dionysius as an enemy from that moment. Hence he continually lived in great danger of being killed by Dionysius' soldiers. But Archytas of Tarentum sent Lamiscus[u] the orator to Dionysius with a ship, asking him to let Plato go. Dionysius released him, giving him provisions, and Plato returned home.

Shortly afterwards Dionysius paid the penalty for his crime committed against philosophy, being driven from his seat of tyranny by Dion and the people. Plato was welcomed back[v] to his own country in high honour. There he was invited to enter the service of the state, but was unwilling to accept, as the people had accustomed themselves to evil ways.

Those to whom Plato gave laws

It is said that the Arcadians and Thebans, who had established a state of respectable size, asked him to set it up as a republic; but when he understood that they were unwilling to pursue the ideal of equality, he did not proceed.[18] However, he did give laws to the Syracusans when the tyrant had been driven out;[19] and for the Cre-

tans he wrote Laws, arranged in twelve books, soon after the city
of Magnesia had been founded.

From those closest to him he sent Aristonymus, to instruct the
Arcadians in the laws; he sent Phormio to the Ilians and Menede-
mus[w] to the Pyrrheans.[20]

Plato's self-restraint, dignity and affability

He lived single. His life was wholly temperate and, as St. Augustine
asserts,[x] chaste. Hence in old age he is said to have made sacrifice
to Nature to free himself, in the view of the people, from the charge[y]
of childlessness.[21] As a young man he had such a sense of propriety
and such composure that he was never caught laughing except mod-
estly.[22] But no one saw him angry. Hence, when a boy who had
been educated under Plato, returned[z] to his parents and saw his
father shouting, he said, 'Never did I see this with Plato.'[23] Only
once was he inwardly somewhat angry with a boy who was doing
serious wrong, but he said to Xenocrates, 'You beat[aa] this boy, for
I cannot, as I am angry'.[24]

No matter what the day he would eat only once or, if twice, very
sparingly. He used to sleep alone. He would strongly condemn a
contrary way of life.[25]

Like his own Socrates too, he seemed somewhat inclined to the
loving of youths; but, in the same measure as both were disposed
to the sensuous, they were restrained by reason. How spiritual was
their love and how what they said about love may be expounded,[bb]
we have dealt with adequately in our book On Love.[26]

Plato chose to bequeath a memorial of himself, both in his books
and in his friends.[27] Although as Aristotle writes[28] he was melancholy
and of a profound nature, yet he used to make many jests, and he
frequently reminded the rather austere Xenocrates and Dion to sacrifice to the Graces so that they would be made more agreeable,[cc]
and gracious.[29] Plato's affability, however, was combined with dignity.

The leading pupils of Plato[30]

His pupils were: Speusippus of Athens, Xenocrates of Chalcedon,
Aristotle of Stagira, Philip of Opus, Hestiaeus of Perinthus, Dion
of Syracuse, Amyclus of Heraclea,[dd] Erastus and Coriscus of Scepsis,

Timolaus of Cyzicus, Euaeon of Lampsacus, Python and Heraclides of Aenus, Hippothales and Callippus of Athens, Demetrius of Amphipolis, Heraclides of Pontus, and several others, among them two women, Lastheneia of Mantinea and Axiothea of Phlius, who both wore men's clothes. It is said that Theophrastus, too, heard him speak, as did Hyperides, the orator, and Chamaeleon and Lycurgus; Demosthenes and Mnesistratus too were devoted to him.[31]

At the entrance to the Academy was inscribed: 'No one lacking geometry may enter here'; which, indeed, he wished to be understood as not only the due measurement of lines but the due measure of the state of mind as well.[32]

Plato's books[33]

He wrote a book, *Euthyphro*, on holiness; he wrote *The Apologia* of Socrates; *Crito*, on what Crito discussed with Socrates in prison; *Phaedo*, on the immortality of the soul; *Cratylus*, on the proper consideration of names; *Theaetetus*, on knowledge; *The Sophist*, on being; *The Statesman*, on government; *Parmenides*, on the single origin of all things and on the ideal forms; *Philebus*, on the highest good; *The Symposium*,[ee] on love; *Phaedrus*, on beauty; *Alcibiades* I, on the nature of man; *Alcibiades* II, on prayer; *Hipparchus*, on the desire for gain; *Amatores*, on philosophy; *Theages*, on wisdom; *Charmides*, on temperance; *Laches*, on courage; *Lysis*,[ff] on friendship; the refutative dialogue *Euthydemus*; *Protagoras*, on ethics; *Gorgias*, on rhetoric; *Meno*, on virtue; *Hippias Maior*, on beauty; *Hippias Minor*, on falsehood; *Menexenus*, on ancient Attica; ten books on *The Republic*; *Timaeus*, on the nature of the universe; *Critias*, on ancient Attica; *Minos*, on law; twelve books on *The Laws; Epinomis*, called The Philosopher; and thirteen *Epistles*.[34] We ourselves have translated all these books of Plato from Greek into Latin.

There are three kinds of Platonic dialogue; that is to say, in one he refutes the sophists, in another he encourages the youth and in the third he teaches adults.[35] What Plato himself says in his letters or his books on *The Laws*, and in *Epinomis*,[gg] he wishes to be taken as completely true; whereas what he discusses through the mouths of Socrates, Timaeus, Parmenides and Zeno, in other books[hh] is to be taken as probable.[36]

The eloquence, wisdom and authority of Plato

The style of Plato (as Aristotle says) flows midway between prose and poetry,[37] and is of such sweetness and fulness that Cicero said that Plato was the greatest authority and master, both in understanding and teaching.[38] He added that if Jupiter had wished to speak with a human tongue he would have spoken with none other than the tongue of Plato. Indeed such great teaching was in him that whereas before him all enlightened Greeks had travelled abroad to foreign peoples[ii] for wisdom's sake, after the time of Plato all nations streamed as one into Athens; even Aristotle, endowed with such wonderful natural abilities and eager for a new way of thinking, listened to Plato's words for twenty years continuously, although he was nearly adult when he came to him.[39] Added to which, before he came to Plato he was already advanced in his studies; from then on he had only Plato as a teacher. Let me quote what Cicero writes:[jj] 'I prefer to err with Plato than to feel I am right with everyone else.'[40] Further, with Panaetius, he calls him the God of philosophers.[41] And Quintilian writes, 'Who doubts that Plato is foremost both in the penetration of his argument and in the divine and Homeric eloquence of his speech, for his language rises so far above the prosaic and what Greeks call "pedestrian" speech, that to me he seems to be instinct not with human genius but with Delphic utterance?'[42] Through godly wisdom[kk] and uprightness he seems to have obtained for himself a wonderful authority, even in his own country, which very rarely happens.

When on his return from Sicily, Plato arrived at that most magnificent assembly of the Olympic Games, which seemed like a gathering of the whole world, he was received with such joyful greetings from all it was as though a god had been sent from heaven to mortal men.[43] You would have seen[ll] the games deserted, the athletic contests abandoned, the boxers left to themselves; and what is more remarkable, people who had come such long journeys over land and sea to feast their eyes, ears and minds on the Olympic games,[mm] forgetful now of all pleasure, were coming to Plato and gazing upon him. In Plato, as in a most delightful hospice, they found their rest.[nn]

When a man was reciting a tragedy with no one[oo] present but Plato, some objected that it was degrading for him that only one person should be there. He replied, 'But this one man is more than the whole Athenian people.'[44]

The charity, magnanimity and holiness of Plato

How great and constant he was in spirit, particularly in the cause of his friends, is shown[pp] by his letters, his contempt for a tyrant and his defence of Dion. Often Plato argued boldly with the tyrant, even in the presence of witnesses, since he said the tyrant governed unjustly and deceived his own friends;[45] so far was Plato from flattering him.[qq] Let me add some minor details, thus: at a feast, Dionysius had ordered everyone to dance dressed in purple. Aristippus promptly danced but Plato declined, saying that women's things did not become a philosopher.[46] Further, the corrupt accuser[rr] Crobylus had laid an accusation against the courageous general Chabrias and had threatened him with sentence of death. In these circumstances, when the general, deserted by all the other citizens and fearing danger, went up into the fortress, only Plato stood by him all the time, ready to give help. The slanderer Crobylus, to prevent him from defending Chabrias, said threateningly, 'You press forward to assist the defence of other people, not heeding that the poison of Socrates awaits you too.' Plato replied, 'In days gone by, Crobylus, when I fought for the honour of my country, I was not slow to face dangers which had to be borne.[ss] Now, for duty and for the safety of a friend I will not turn from any crisis, even though you may threaten sword, poison and fire.'[47]

When Socrates had been imprisoned most unjustly, Plato collected money to buy the release of the innocent man, and while the trial was in progress, he ascended the platform and began to speak thus: 'O men of Athens,[tt] although I am younger than all those here who have mounted the tribunal . . .' then the tyrannical judges,[uu] fearing that his authority and eloquence might move the citizens, suddenly interrupted and shouted, 'Get down!'[48] Plato left for home. For he was then suffering from some bodily sickness, just as they were suffering from sickness of the mind.[vv] In fact, Socrates' persecutors paid the penalty soon afterwards.

One of the fellow-disciples of Xenocrates was pricked by jealousy that Xenocrates was so favoured and so close to Plato. In order to arouse hostility against Xenocrates, he reported many malicious sayings of Xenocrates against Plato.[ww] Plato listened but rejected the charge as he was speaking. The malicious critic stood his ground, with hardened countenance, affirming the charge. At length, Plato, to free himself from the tenacity of the man who was calling on all the gods and goddesses to bear witness, said, 'Be it so: but Xenocrates is so strong in faith and is of such dignity that unless he had judged it to be useful he would never have said these things.'[49]

Diogenes' *Life of Xenocrates*[50] bears witness that Xenocrates, the beloved disciple of Plato, imitated his dignity and magnanimity; and Xenocrates' life is indeed an example of fortitude and devotion. Plutarch is a witness that Dion too imitated Plato.[51] Further, Philiscus,[52] describing the life of the orator Lycurgus, says, 'Lycurgus was a great man, and many things were brilliantly accomplished by him which no man could have done who had not been a pupil of Plato.'

When fleeing from Antipater, Demosthenes said to Archias, who was promising to save his life with fawning words, 'Far be it from me that, after I have heard both Xenocrates and Plato discoursing on the immortality of the soul, I should prefer to live with shame rather than to die with honour.'[53] The same man, writing to a certain Heracleodorus, his fellow student, reproached him because, after he had listened to Plato, he neglected good studies and led a life of little honour. He said, 'Do you not feel ashamed to be neglecting what you have learned from Plato?'[54]

Dionysius, writing to Speusippus says, 'Plato used to teach without charge those who frequented his house, but you exact fees, and take them from those who are willing to pay and those who are not.'[55] Laertius also criticises Speusippus for not, in contrast to Xenocrates, imitating Plato's purity, fortitude and gentleness.[56]

I cannot be silent about Xenocrates' courage when Dionysius said to Plato, 'Someone will take off your head.' Xenocrates, who was there, said, 'No one cuts off[xx] that head without first cutting off mine!'[57]

Maxims and sayings of Plato[58]

Plato used to say this about Aristotle and Xenocrates, 'Oh![yy] What have I taken on to be yoked together! A horse and an ass! Aristotle needs the bridle, but Xenocrates needs the spur.'[59]

There was amongst his disciples an over-fastidious young man, too concerned about his external appearance: Plato asked him, 'How long will you go on building a prison for yourself?'

As often as he might see a man ensnared by love he used to say, 'That man is dead in his own body; he lives in another's.' He would add, 'He who deserts his own self for the sake of another is of all men the most miserable, since he no longer possesses either himself or the other.'

A certain close friend of Plato, a learned man, was pleading with Plato to listen for a while as he was intent on reading a paper he had produced. Whereupon, asked by Plato what was the title of the work, he answered, 'Do not contradict.' Plato said to him, 'Why then are you doing so yourself? Why contradict contradictors? Why consult me since you do not allow yourself to be contradicted?'[60]

A powerful citizen, Leo, was publicly criticised for making a loud and excessive uproar in the senate. Plato said, 'This is truly being a lion.'

To Diogenes the Cynic who maintained that he certainly saw mortal things but ideas not at all, Plato said, 'What a marvel![zz] For you have eyes with which these mortal things are seen, and you use them, but you do not use the mind by which alone ideas[ab] are discerned.'[61]

To some disciples, marvelling that Xenocrates, throughout his life a grave man,[cb] had said something intended to be received with laughter, Plato said, 'What? Do you wonder that amongst thorns sometimes roses and lilies are born?'

To young men[db] he often used to say, 'Put work before leisure, unless perhaps you think rust better than brilliance.'

He used to fire[eb] the young with enthusiasm for a happy life, very often with this reasoning: 'Consider the contrary nature of virtue and pleasure: for the momentary sweetness of the latter is followed by sudden[fb] remorse and perpetual sorrow; but the brief toils of the former are followed by eternal delight.'[62]

When he saw someone playing at dice Plato rebuked him, and when the man said, 'What small matters you find fault with!' Plato replied, 'On the contrary! Habit is no small matter.'[63]

He used to advise drunkards and those prone to rage to observe themselves attentively in a mirror; they would immediately turn their backs on^{gb} such foulness.[64] Drunkenness and idleness he abhorred.

He used to say that in the education of the young what is of most importance is that children should become accustomed to delight only in those things that are honourable. 'Otherwise,' he used to say, 'pleasure is a bait for evils.'[65] He would add that true health of mind is love of wisdom. In truth other powers seem to be not so much love of wisdom as embellishments. Nothing is sweeter for a healthy mind than to speak and hear true things; for there is nothing better or more enduring than truth.[66] To some people who asked what kind of possessions then should one chiefly provide for one's children, he said, 'Those which would dread neither hailstorm, nor the violence of men nor even Jove himself.'

To Demodocus,^{hb} taking counsel about the instruction of his son, Plato said, 'There should be the same care in the begetting and rearing of children as there is in the planting and training of young trees. The rearing is work, the begetting pleasure; but beware lest we seem deeply asleep at the work yet more than awake in the pleasure.'

To a certain Philedon, who was carping^{ib} at Plato because Plato was no less zealous and assiduous in learning than in teaching, and who was asking him how long he wished to be a student, Plato said, 'For as long as I have no cause to repent being better and wiser.'

Asked what was the difference between a wise man and an ignorant man, he replied, 'The difference between a doctor and a sick man.'

He used to say that for princes there was no more excellent kind of surety for men in their position than to have retainers to whom trade was unknown.[67]

He said, 'To the prince wisdom is as necessary as breath to the body. States will be most blessed if either philosophers rule or at least, by some divine destiny, those who govern study philosophy; for nothing is a greater scourge than power and boldness which are accompanied by ignorance. Also, subjects are usually such as they see their princes to be.[68]

'A magistrate should consider not his own but the public good; not some part only, but the whole of the state, should be his care.'

How lightly Plato regarded the human; how much he delighted in the divine

Every day he used to repeat, 'The eternal alone is true, the temporal only seems to be.[jb] The soul sleeps in the body and those things that the senses desire or fear are nothing but dreams. Thus all such things are to be thoroughly contemned, and to avoid the evils which are plentiful in the world we must flee to the eternal for refuge. For in no other way can evils be avoided.'[69]

And he put into practice what he taught. For when,[kb] both by an hereditary right and the support of the citizens, he would have been a leader in the state, he totally rejected all public honour. When by inheritance from his father he became very rich, he showered all on his brothers, except for a small suburban estate, called Academia.[70] With this alone he lived content. Although he came to be the teacher and the friend of princes, yet he accepted no riches from them. King Dionysius used to say, 'Aristippus is always asking for money, Plato is always asking for books.'[71] In addition be neither took a wife nor lived in the city. Free from all things, he served truth alone.

Whence, St. Jerome says, 'Despite great difficulties Plato travelled throughout Egypt, and to Archytas of Tarentum and to that coast of Italy formerly called Magna Graecia. So that he who in Athens was a master and a man of power, with whose teaching the halls of the Academy resounded, became a pilgrim and a disciple, preferring humbly to learn from the words of others rather than, without modesty, to hold forth himself.

'Finally while pursuing[lb] learning which seemed to flee before him round the whole globe, he was captured by pirates and sold into slavery; furthermore he served the cruellest tyrant. Captive, bound and enslaved, yet, because a philosopher, he was greater than the man buying him.'[72] Thus Jerome.

The piety and gratitude of Plato

He was filled with gratitude to God, from whom, he used to say, the beginning of thinking, speaking and acting in all matters ought to be made;[73] and he himself always put this into practice. Moreover, he gave thanks daily to God that he was born a man and not a brute, that he was born a Greek and not a barbarian, and that he was born in the time of Socrates.[74] His dialogues, in which he wonderfully honours his teachers and all his friends, are testimony to how grateful he was to them all. And he ascribed his books to Socrates; for not only does he introduce him as disputant in almost all his dialogues, but also writes[mb] that everything he had set down was not his but Socrates'.[75]

What Plato affirmed and those who[nb] supported him

In matters subject to the senses he used to support the views of Heraclitus. Then in that which pertains to the intellect he would rest mainly with Pythagoras. But in matters affecting the community he embraced his own Socrates.[76]

These are the things which he asserted everywhere: God provides for all; the souls of men are immortal; there will be rewards for the good, punishments for the wicked.[77]

Augustine, in his book *Against the Academics*, says, 'The authority of Christ must be put before everything.' However, if there is something to be done requiring the use of reason, he says he finds himself with the Platonists, for this is not contrary to the sacred Christian writings.[78] Dionysius the Areopagite[79] pointed out the same; later Eusebius and Cyril[80] explained it more fully. Hence Augustine, in his book *On True Religion* says, 'If a few things were changed, the Platonists would become Christians.'[81] And in *The Confessions* he relates that he has found nearly all the opening words of John the Evangelist in the works of the Platonists.[82] Therefore in the second book of *The City of God* he says, 'Labeo the pagan theologian thought that Plato should be numbered with the demigods, like Hercules and Romulus. Furthermore, he places demigods above heroes. But both he sets among the divine powers. Nevertheless I have no doubt that Plato, whom he calls a demigod, should be preferred[ob] not only to the heroes but even to the gods themselves.'[83] Whence he says that he chose the Platonists before other philosophers as they had a much truer understanding of divine and human matters than the rest. Also Marcus Varro[84] had earlier come to this conclusion and Apuleius regarded Plato as not merely superior to the heroes but equal to the gods, since he had evidently penetrated the inmost secrets[pb] of divine matters.[85]

Plato was endowed with such modesty that, although he had won himself marvellous authority above others, even so, when he was asked by someone for how long his precepts should be obeyed he replied, 'Until someone holier appear on earth to uncover the fountain of truth for all; whom in the end all will follow.'[86]

He added that he had discovered[qb] nothing by his own light but much by divine light. However, what he observed in philosophy we have discussed adequately in our books, *On Love* and *The Theology*.

Plato's return to his celestial land and praises of him

It was on his birthday that he departed life, when he had fulfilled eighty-one years and not a day less. For this reason the Magi who were then in Athens made sacrifice to Plato; they reckoned his lot to be greater than that of a human being since he had fulfilled the most perfect number, which is the product of nine times nine.[87] And, what is a marvel, he was still writing at that age and on that very day; about which Cicero says, 'There is also the calm and gentle[rb] old age of a quiet and pure life lived with good judgement; such we are told was that of Plato who died while writing at eighty-one years[sb] of age.'[88] Seneca also affirms that Plato[tb] reached this age by means of even-mindedness and care.[89] Some affirm that he returned to the gods above while writing, others that he returned in mid-discourse, while reclining after the meal had been cleared at a wedding feast.[90]

Aristotle consecrated an altar and a statue to Plato in a temple with this inscription: βωμον Ἀριστοτελης ἱδρυσατο Τονδε Πλατωνος ὁν ἐπαινουν Τοισι Κακοισι Θεμις[ub], that is, 'Aristotle has dedicated this altar to Plato, a man[vb] whom it is sacrilege for bad men to praise.'[91] Aristotle added, 'By his life, his teaching, his conduct and his speech, he alone gave guidance to all men, and handed on his writings, so that through virtue they might be able to lead a happy life. No future age will bring forth such a man.'[92] And other wise men have added many verses to the praise of Plato, but above all[wb] three epitaphs.[93] This is the meaning of the first: 'He excelled all men in temperance and justice, but was so far above them in wisdom that he completely overcame[xb] all envy.' This is the sense of the second: 'Plato has been removed from the world to be numbered among the gods; distant nations honour him, for he had knowledge himself of the divine life, and showed it to others.'

The third sentence is like this: 'Phoebus begat Aesculapius and Plato—Aesculapius to heal bodies, Plato to heal souls.'[94]

Furthermore, Mithridates, the King of the Persians, placed in the Academy a statue of Plato with this inscription: 'Mithridates, the Persian, son of Orontobates, has dedicated this image of Plato (the work of Silanion) to the Muses.'[95]

From all this Plato attained such a reputation that, although the Greeks placed Aristotle among the spirits, they named Plato divine; because it is clear that, in the main, Aristotle's life was earthly, and his knowledge natural; whereas Plato, at once by knowledge and by his life, devoted himself above all to the divine.

An Apologia on the character of Plato

I shall now draw to a close, once I have added a few more words.

There are some common rhymesters[yb] who without meriting it, usurp for themselves the name of poet. Roused as much by the difference in conduct as by the malice of envy, they mock shamelessly any man of excellence. And to these men a certain supreme licence is allowed against good men rather than bad, especially in our time.[96] But let me not be mindful of our times, which are as incapable of pursuing virtue as they seem to be well capable of persecuting it. Accordingly, in former times, such petty poets did not hesitate to sink their teeth into the divine Plato, considered by the Greeks to be the son of Apollo, and also into Socrates, considered by Apollo to be the wisest of Greeks. Diogenes Laertius utterly detested the impiety of these poets. And, as Diogenes declares, Aristippus of Cyrene, the most wicked man of his time and an adversary of the best one[zb] of his time, also added to the facetious abuse of the comic poets.[97] Just as Aristippus slandered many other very virtuous and learned men with false stories, so he even slandered Socrates his teacher and his own fellow pupils, Xenophon[98] and Plato. He made up[ac] certain lascivious poems in their names about harlots and young boys,[99] evidently so that, by falsely using the great philosophers as examples, he might procure a freer licence to sin himself.

But Aristotle, to whom truth was more dear than Plato,[100] could not tolerate such false calumny against a holy man. For in his elegies to Eudemus he recites those words about Plato which we have quoted above, paying him the greatest tribute: that profane men not only must not slander Plato in any way, but even, under the pretext[bc] of praise, they should not dare to utter his holy name through their profane mouths.[101] And he was not content with an elegy, but also, according to Olympiodorus, composed a brilliant oration in praise of Plato.[102]

Therefore let the hounds of hell be silent in the world of the living; rather let them howl in company with Cerberus in the world of the dead. But, for our part, let us venerate Plato's life and wisdom, in the judgement of the wise[dc] regarded as the best, and together with Apuleius of Madaura let us freely proclaim: 'We, the family of Plato, know nothing except what is bright, joyful, celestial and supreme.'[103]

20

Quantum astronomi metiuntur, tantum astrologi mentiuntur

To the very degree that astronomers measure, astrologers misrepresent

Marsilio Ficino to Bernardo Bembo, the distinguished lawyer and knight: greetings.

A THOUSAND blessings upon you, my Bernardo. But I have not uttered enough; a blessing upon you with each breath, sweetest Bernardo. Though I write a great many words to you every day, I transcribe few. For when I have written the original I seem, in some measure, to have satisfied love; nay, if I were to transcribe from duty, I would give very little satisfaction.

But now to inform you of our present studies: I am composing a book on the providence of God and the freedom of human will,[1] in which I refute, to the best of my ability, those pronouncements of the astrologers which remove providence and freedom. Indeed, as carefully as true[a] astronomers measure the heavens, so do vain astrologers misrepresent human affairs. Farewell.

Most idle hand, why do you neglect for so long to mention that true and illustrious Tommaso,[2] Achates of that Bernardo who was once Venetian Ambassador; Tommaso, whom my soul gladly embraces and my tongue magnifies? So, Bernardo, as often as you see him, greet him in Marsilio's name.

14th June, 1477.

21

Tunc maxime commendas aliquem, cum ostendis illius esse, cui commendas

You commend someone most highly when you show him to belong to the one to whom you make the commendation

Marsilio Ficino to Marco Aurelio, the illustrious orator: greetings.

IF it were in order to commend to you what is your own, I should very strongly commend to you Niccolo, a member of my household, who is endowed with both education and character. That he is indeed your own is shown to us by your name, which very frequently sounds on his lips.

22

Quando divino afflante spiritu amor accenditur, saemper
amante altero redamat alter. Saepe altero cogitante, idem
cogitat alter

Since love is kindled by the breath of a divine spirit,
when one loves, the other always returns love; often
when one thinks, the other thinks the same

Marsilio Ficino to Bernardo Bembo, the distinguished lawyer[a] and
knight: greetings.

BERNARDO, I have today received from[b] our Marco Aurelio a letter,
which even in its very form is entirely Mercurial, and in all respects
similar to its father; yet, I judge it to have been born with Saturn in
the ascendant. Certainly, it has been moving with rather ponderous
steps, since it left Venetian waters[c] on the sixteenth of May and
finally reached our shores on the nineteenth of June. Clasping it
with utmost joy, I congratulate it: 'You have come at last, and your
devotion has overcome the hard journey.'[1]

Although it appeared to be rather slow in its motion, as if born
under Saturn, it is seen to have been very swift in its work, as if
conceived by Mercury. For what it asks of us today, it has itself
long since fulfilled, while being born. Indeed, in those same[d] days
of May, when the golden Aurelio wrote to me, I, moved by some
mysterious and well-nigh divine impulse, either from his letter or
his Muse, dedicated to Aurelio a little work,[2] which, I think, unless
also Saturnine in its pace, will already have reached you.

Bernardo, just consider the wonderful[e] power of our guardian
spirits; while that Marco was giving himself freely to me, I in return,
in obedience to the law, was giving myself wholly to him; and—
cause of wonder—as he with love was taking hold of me, I was
encompassing him. And so, by the breath of a heavenly spirit, we
have simultaneously and, almost unknowingly, breathed as one.
Indeed, I judge that either Mercury himself, positioned in Taurus,
or Phoebus in Gemini has tuned alike the twin lyres of Aurelio and
Marsilio, so that with the sounding of one the other in turn resounds.

And from both, that sweet name of Bembo reverberates, a name musical to the Graces and most gratifying to the Muses.

Fare prosperously.

But I see that my Bernardo—for I have come to know the man's nature—is neither able nor willing ever to fare well without those in whom he delights: Cristoforo Landino, a man worthy of Minerva and the Muses, and our fellow philosopher Giovanni Cavalcanti, fare well. And so farewell.

19 June, 1477.

23

Quando divino afflante spiritu amor accenditur, saemper amante altero redamat alter, saepe altero cogitante, idem cogitat[a] alter

Since love is kindled by the breath of a divine spirit, when one loves, the other always returns love; often when one thinks, the other thinks the same

Marsilio Ficino of Florence to Marco Aurelio, the illustrious orator: greetings.

YOUR elegant letter was delivered to us yesterday, most learned Marco; a letter sweeter to me than honey and more precious than gold. But what am I to do? It is not lawful for me to proceed further with this praise, lest I seem too vain in attempting myself to praise sufficiently a letter which praises me more than sufficiently. So, if you please, let us begin again from another point.

Since love is kindled in our hearts by the breath of some celestial spirit, when one loves, the other always returns love; and often when one is thinking, the other is thinking the same thing in the same way. For since the heavenly father, as the common cause of all things, enfolds both, he creates the mutual love of the lovers; and the love of the lover proceeding[b] from heaven through man, reflects back, now in the earthly face of humanity, then in the vaults of heaven: in turn, it gives birth to Echo.[1]

So welcome, heavenly friend, welcome always in God, the author of our friendship;[c] neither distance on earth nor span of time, Marco, seem to have been able to interrupt the rise, or retard the course, of this our heavenly, perpetual love. No, by a divine bond, when one loves, soon the other shall love; moreover when one thinks and writes, at almost the same moment the other will think and write the same. I think you will have observed, Aurelio, if you have received that little work of mine[2] recently sent to you, that at the very time you were writing to me, I in turn was also writing to you; furthermore, that each of us signalled inwardly[d] and then asked for the same thing.

For me nothing is more fruitful in human affairs than through love to have become equal to one whom, as I am aware, no one excels in virtue. Nothing is more precious than so fortunately to possess one of such quality and stature as my possessor. So I have what I was seeking with my whole heart.

But I am somewhat troubled in this one respect, that I am by no means wholly that which you yourself were seeking. If you cannot have what you may desire, my Aurelio, may you at least desire what you can have. Accept your Marsilio whole, Marco, however short he may be. Look no further I beg you at that image which you had initially imagined, for Ficino is a limb of that image. Look at what you possess, my friend, rather than at what you imagine. Thus you will certainly realise you possess not part of anything but something whole. It is better to enjoy a whole pigmy rather than a limb of some huge giant.

24

Nihil infirmius quam humanus amor, nihil firmius quam
divinus

*Nothing is less constant than human love, nothing more
constant than divine love*

Marsilio Ficino to Bernardo Bembo, lawyer and illustrious knight:
greetings.

You write to us an eloquent, poetic and loving letter; however, I
do not know why you are needlessly making excuses, because ab-
solutely no one is making accusations. Where love is perfect, beware
lest you believe that any tiny offence can ever touch it. You can
perhaps harm love in only one way; by believing that love can ever
be harmed.

Human love is indeed a condition which is full of unceasing
agitation and fear.[1] But, if we listen to Paul, divine love 'believeth
all things, hopeth all things, endureth all things, and never faileth;'[2]
or to John the Evangelist, 'There is no fear in love, but perfect love
casteth out all fear.'[3] Hence our own St. Augustine exclaims, 'Only
he never loses any beloved one, for whom all are beloved in that
one who is never lost.'[4]

But I do not know how I came at this point to begin a homily,
as it is called, and[a] was propounding the offices of love to the man
whom the people of Florence revere as an image of love, and a
model of humanity.

25

Frustra nimium in rebus his quae sibimet nequaquam sufficiunt, nostram sufficientiam affectamus

Vainly and to excess we strive for our satisfaction in those things which in no wise satisfy themselves

Marsilio Ficino to Mankind: greetings.

YOU seek satisfaction everywhere, on the principle that after you have found this one thing, you will search for nothing further.[a] But you are always seeking anew as many things as possible, for the very reason that nowhere do you attain this one thing. So do you wish me to say why you attain satisfaction nowhere? Perhaps because it is outside yourself that you are seeking. If, therefore, mortal possessions cannot satisfy the immortal soul, at least take care that the soul itself may give satisfaction to mortal things. Mark what I say. I do not say that the soul should satisfy itself, for how can that which is formed and perfected by another satisfy itself?[b] Alas, pitiable creatures, how much wasted effort! We seek our satisfaction in those things which in no wise satisfy themselves. In truth, only that which satisfies itself, satisfies all things wholly. Nothing, however, can satisfy[c] itself, but the immeasurable good which comes from itself and returns to itself. Here alone then, here, I say, we should seek that which will satisfy us. Nor would this bring regret, for no one ever follows the good in vain, who follows it truly. For the good itself being without measure, blooms and comes forth in abundance from every point; and our desire[d] to follow it truly is without doubt something good. But he alone truly desires and follows the good who, by grace of the supreme good itself, through which individual good things have their being and are preserved, follows at every step individual things that are good.[1]

26

Transitus repentinus a minimo lumine ad maximum, atque a
maximo ad minimum, aciem impedit

*A sudden transition from the least light to the greatest,
and also from the greatest to the least, blunts the keen
edge of vision*

Marsilio Ficino to Riccardo Angiolieri, the distinguished theologian
from Anghiari.

MEN engaged in civil life often speak out against philosophers because they seem, for the most part, ill-fitted for the government of
human affairs. Philosophers in return condemn even more frequently those engaged in civil affairs for being totally unfit for
contemplation of the divine. So what shall we ourselves say about
this? It is not for us to settle disputes of such magnitude between
these men.[1] But our Plato, whom God Himself especially prepared
for both human and divine matters, should be summoned here as
arbiter. Accordingly, he observes that from the beginning both men
of affairs and philosophers have been ordained to fulfil either office.
If only they would not move suddenly from one extreme to the
other, but step by step.[2] Here it is best to translate Plato's Greek
itself, word for word, from the seventh book of *The Republic*.[3]
    'And now you may contemplate our nature with respect to learn-
ing and ignorance by such an image as this. Imagine an underground
cave; its entrance, facing an incipient light, gives access to the entire
cave, affording a passage through from every direction; in it are
men reared from childhood, bound neck and leg so that they are
forced to remain immobile and to look only to the front; they cannot
even turn their heads, bound as they are with chains. And behind
their backs high[a] and far off hangs a fiery torch. Between this fire
and the bound men runs a raised path, alongside which a low wall
has been built. It is like the stage or curtain which puppet-masters
feigning miracles often place before the eyes of spectators and above
which they demonstrate their wonders. Now imagine men beneath
the wall bearing various vessels and man-made objects which show

above the wall;[b] statues of men and images of different animals fashioned in various ways from stone and wood. And as you might expect, some of those who bear these things are silent and some are speaking.

'Like ourselves are those bound men. For, firstly, do you think they see anything at all of themselves or of the men nearest them, except shadows cast by the fire upon the opposite side of the cave? And of those objects[c] which are being carried about do they not see merely shadows? So if they were allowed to speak with one another, would they not express the opinion[d] that those things which they saw facing them were speaking? Suppose an echo were to ring out from the opposite side of the dungeon whenever one of those passing behind spoke, do you not think they would believe that it was but the shadows of the things passing across that spoke? In every way, therefore, such men would consider there was nothing true except shadows of man-made objects.

'Now consider on the other hand what the release from their bonds and the remedy for their ignorance would be like. No doubt if one of them were to be released and forced to rise suddenly, to turn his neck, walk and look towards the light itself, he would immediately be in pain and not be able, on account of the brilliance, to look upon those things whose shadows he had previously seen. What, then, if someone were to tell him that he had hitherto gazed at illusions, and that he was now closer to real things and was perceiving them more accurately? What if someone, pointing to one of those passing by, were to ask what it was? Do you not think that he would be confused and believe that those things which he had seen previously were more real than those which were now being shown? And if someone forced[e] him to look at the light, do you not think that he would be stricken with pain in his eyes? And would he not cast his eyes back to those things which before he had seen with ease, counting them to be more sure than those which were suddenly presented? Indeed, if anyone were to drag him violently upward through rough, steep places, not allowing him to look at anything before dragging him to the light of the sun, do you not think that he would bear it ill while being torn away?[f] And when he had been led forth to the light, his eyes suffused with the brilliance, would he not be at a loss and see none of those things which are now considered real by men?

'He therefore needs first to accustom himself, if he is going to look at things above, and in the beginning he will look more easily upon shadows. After this he will more readily behold the reflections of men and other things in water; next objects themselves, and then those things which are in the sky; and he will behold the heaven itself more easily by night, whilst he observes the light of the stars and moon, than if he were to look by day at the sun itself and the full brightness of its light.

'And thus at length he will raise his eyes to the sun itself, not looking at images of it in water, and in places[g] other than its own, but observing it itself in accordance with itself, in its proper place, and he will be able to recognise it as it is.[h] He will at length perceive that it is this which regulates the seasons and years, which rules all things under heaven and is in some way the author of whatever was previously seen by him and his fellows. What if he returns in memory to the original habitation and the wisdom of those men and the fetters? Do you not think that he would count himself blessed in his change of place, and yet pity those others? If they, moreover, presented honours and praise to each other and rewards were given to him who was sharp in discerning any of the passing objects, who recollected most fully which ones were wont to go before, which after and which together, and from these best predicted what was to come; do you suppose that he himself would long for these things and would consider those men happy who were honoured and dominant amongst them?

'Or would he not, as Homer says,[4] choose a fate in a foreign land, even that of being made slave to another slave on a country estate and enduring no matter what else, rather than be fooled by such beliefs and live in such wretchedness?

'If he descends again and takes up the same seat as before, will he not be overcome[i] by the darkness, since he has so suddenly parted from the sun? And if it is necessary to distinguish between those shadows and make judgements[j] about them with the men held fast by perpetual fetters; if an opinion has to be offered at the very time[k] when his eyes are full of darkness, and before his vision has cleared, which indeed will not happen in a short time, will he not excite derision? And dishonour will be imputed to him by all because, after ascending to the upper regions, he has returned with his eyesight ruined; and it will be said that one should never strive towards the upper realm, and whoever tries to release another and lead him upwards is, if caught, to be killed instantly.

'This entire allegory, my friend, should be related to our previous discussion. Thus our dungeon relates to that[l] fabric of the world which is discerned by the eyes, whilst the light of the fire in the cave refers to the power of the sun.[m] Finally, you will not be mistaken if you compare, as I hope you will, the ascent towards the upper realms, and the vision of them, to that ascent which is directed towards the world of intellect.

'Since you desire to hear my opinion, God knows if it be true, this is how it appears to me. As I judge, beyond any doubt the idea of the good itself stands supreme in the world of intellect and is seen with difficulty. Yet if it is seen, it must be asserted that in all things it is the cause of all that is right and good, since, in the visible region, it has itself created light and the source of light, and reigning in the world of intellect, it has brought forth truth and mind.

'And it is necessary that the whole idea of the good be known by anyone[n] who with right mind is to undertake any action either privately or in public.

'Well now, consider this and do not be surprised[o] that those who come down to this place do not want to handle human affairs, but rather always direct the keen edge of their mind to the world above. Indeed, this is[p] most probable if we follow the former allegory. Furthermore, why should you marvel if one who has come down from the sight of divine wonders to these human ills, is less capable of acting and is ridiculed; especially if, before he becomes accustomed to the present darkness and while still reeling, he is forced to give evidence in courts of law or elsewhere about the shadows of what is lawful or the statues which[q] cast these shadows, and to discuss the judgments of those who have never seen justice herself? Yet, any man of reason will remember that the eyes may be confused in two ways and from two causes: firstly, when we come down from light to shadow and secondly, when we go forth from darkness into sunlight. He will deem the mind to be affected in the same way, whenever he sees it confused and slower at distinguishing any thing. Therefore he will by no means burst thoughtlessly into laughter, but will carefully inquire whether the mind, in descending from a purer existence, has been overwhelmed by unaccustomed darkness

or whether, rising from utter folly to the vision of brilliance, it has
failed beneath such dazzling splendour.

'And indeed he will approve the condition of the mind in the
second instance and judge that its life will be blessed, yet he will
pity[r] it in the first. But if by chance he does begin to laugh, it will
be less out of place for him to laugh at one who is ascending than
at one who has fallen from the light[s] above.'

Thus says the divine Plato, and nothing should be taken away
from these words, nor can anything be added to them.

Therefore, farewell.

27

Quod animus immortalis sit. Atque cur cum sit divinus,
     saepe tamen vitam agit[a] bestiae similem

That the soul is immortal. And why, though it be divine,
it often leads a life similar to that of a beast[1]

Marsilio Ficino to Giovanni Nesi,[b] distinguished by his writings and
conduct: greetings.

WERE[c] there not within us divine power, and were our minds not
of heavenly origin, we could in no way acknowledge the insuffi-
ciency of mortal things and[d] we should certainly never reason beyond, or pursue anything above, the physical level. No one[e] would
exert himself at all, even in the smallest matter, to resist the body
for[f] we should be satisfied with earthly riches. And[g] all men, or
certainly the great majority, would rest content[h] with this middle
region of the universe[2] as their natural birthplace and home. But as
it is, since our condition is very different, I believe—and with no
empty faith—that we are of divine origin. Yet, if we are divine,
why do we often lead a life similar to that of a beast? It is because
the natural condition of this region determines that we use sense like
an animal long before we use reason like men. Furthermore, far
more numerous and more obvious inducements present themselves

to our senses than to our minds. Lastly, the man in us is one, but the beasts are many.

It is worthwhile considering that picture of us which Plato paints in the ninth book of *The Republic*, thus:[3]

'Let us fashion an image of the soul similar to the natures once said to have been possessed by the Chimaera, Scylla, Cerberus and many another, in which, they say, a variety of forms was begotten in one body. So picture a single model of a beast of many forms, having heads facing all directions; some, I say, are the heads of tame beasts and some of wild, all of which it can generate from itself and interchange with each other. Above these add the form of a lion and at the top one of a man. Let the first one described be the largest, the second and third smaller. Then, join these three so that they coalesce to make one. Surround them with the form of a single man, so that to one who is unable to look within but only on the surface, who discerns only the covering, the man seems clearly to be one being.

'Thus to him who asserts that it profits this human being to act unjustly, but that it does not profit him at all to live justly, let us point out that he is asserting just this: that it profits the human being to feed the manifold beast and the lion, and to make them both stronger, but to allow the man to starve and to be so weakened that because of his feebleness he is dragged in whatever direction the other two carry him off. He should not make them gentle or friendly with one another; rather should he allow them as separate creatures to savage one another, and their conflicts to devour them alike.

'Accordingly, the man who declares that just actions[i] are profitable will advise what ought to be said and done to enable the man within a being of this kind to achieve complete mastery. He should tend the many-headed[j] monster like a husbandman, cherishing the tame heads, giving them water and food, but instantly[k] cutting off the wild ones, making the lion's nature his ally in this; and in common care of them all, he should reconcile each one[l] with the others in mutual goodwill towards himself.

'And so, from every consideration, he who praises what is just, speaks truth; but he who praises what is unjust, lies. For in relation to pleasure, honour and advantage, the commender of justice proclaims truth; but he who slanders justice speaks no truth,[m] nor does he know what he condemns.' Thus far Plato.

A similar division of our soul is described in Plato's *Timaeus*.[4]
There he divides the soul into three powers, as into parts, whose
natures are reason, passion and desire. He has appointed the power
of reason to the head, queen, as it were, in the highest citadel, chiefly
because the head more than anything else seems to exert itself in
watching; and it is there that all the senses are most vigorous. Next,
he has set the power of passion in the region of the heart, since it
is in anger, boldness and fear that this region is most agitated. Lastly,
he has given the power of desire to the liver because its natural
vigour lends itself both to the digestion of food and to the growth
of bodily craving.

Likewise in *Phaedrus*[5] he calls reason a charioteer, since in the
order of nature it is master of the other parts. To the charioteer he
links twin horses, one white and one black. As he sees this analogy,
the horses are the powers of the heart and the liver because these
should submit to reason as to a charioteer.[n] Magnanimity, which is
accorded to the heart, is said to be the white horse, for it is closer
to reason. But the liver's power of desire is the black horse, since
it is farther away from the pre-eminence of reason.

Then again, reason within us is called Hercules: he destroys Antaeus,[6] that is the monstrous images of fantasy, when he lifts Antaeus
up from the earth, that is, when he removes himself[o] from the
senses and physical images. He also subdues the lion, meaning that
he curbs passion. He cuts down the Hydra with its many sprouting
heads; that is, he cuts off the force of desire which, as passion, is
borne not into a few things,[p] and those of great importance, but
into anything whatsoever, or rather into innumerable things, by
means of an insatiable whirlpool. But while our Hercules is cutting
down the Hydra of the liver with his sword, heads instantly sprout
again because the fuel for new heads is still there. But when he
consumes the Hydra by fire, he utterly destroys the fuel and so
nothing is born from it again.

In Plato's *Phaedo*, Socrates commands thus: 'Do not abstain from
one bodily pleasure to gratify another. Otherwise in place of the
one, many are instantly reborn.'[7] On the contrary, he enjoins us to
try to abstain from pleasures for the sake of reason, for only thus is
it possible, he says, to root out vices at the source.

Let me now bring this letter to an end, but may I first remind
you of this one thing, which clearly we should bear in mind: if the

wild beasts within us are many,[q] it is not surprising that according to Plato souls are transmigrating from man to beasts.[8] Certainly we have within us, from the beginning, fuel for desire and something of animal nature. When we have heedlessly nourished these for a long time, reason is either in some way lulled to sleep, or else it is awake under a cloak of passion and desire. Wherefore, under that human skin, the man himself seems to have been transformed into beasts. Hence Socrates says in *Phaedrus*, 'Indeed I examine myself, Phaedrus. Am I a monster with more heads than Typhon, more full of fire and fury? Or am I a simpler and calmer being, sharing in some divine and favourable destiny, partaking in a quiet understanding?'[9]

1st July, 1477.

28

Solus omnia possidet qui a nullo, praeter deum, penitus
possidetur

*He alone possesses all things who is inwardly possessed
by nothing but God*

Marsilio Ficino to his beloved[a] fellow priest, Girolamo Pasqualini: greetings.

IF you desire to possess as many things as possible, take care that nothing possesses you within. For unless you have possession of yourself, through whom you may possess other things, you will have nothing at all. Hence it is that all men are always in want, that they all continually grieve, because clearly each of them[b] has for a long time too rashly lost and wasted himself, and everything else with himself. Inwardly each is taken captive,[c] while outwardly he strives to capture. He alone can belong at once to himself and to another, who has given himself to that one alone who, among all things, is alone for this very reason: that he alone is all things. For when a man finds all things in this one, he also^d finds himself, as much more perfect than himself as is that one. Just as he who serves someone in bondage is in bondage,^e in most vile and wretched bondage, so he who serves the Lord of all things becomes in a measure the Lord of all things. He alone seems to serve freely who submits to the will of infinite freedom.

Service is free where boundless freedom, that is, God, casts out whatever may be thought subject to bondage or force.

29

Cum primum fatum impugnare nitimur, expugnamus

As soon as we strive to oppose fate, we overcome it

Marsilio Ficino to Francesco Marescalchi of Ferrara: greetings.

You ask, my excellent fellow philosopher, four questions. Firstly, how am I? Indeed, Marescalchi, I am as I wish to be, since I now wish to be as I am. Secondly, why do I practise philosophy? I practise philosophy chiefly for this reason: since events themselves do not otherwise follow my will, at least I by my will shall follow events, for it is to a will which follows them that events conform. Thirdly, how much do I love you? If there be any measure to love,^a or rather if there be any fixed measure to free will, measure your love towards me, Francesco; thus perhaps you may measure my love towards you. Fourthly, what am I working on? I am preparing a book on the providence of God and the freedom of human judgement,¹ in which a case is moved against the predetermination of the stars and the prophetic utterances of the astrologers.

But perhaps someone may say it is foolish to wish to contend against unassailable fate. I, however, reply that it can be opposed as easily as one may wish to oppose it, since by that very opposition one may immediately overcome what one wishes. Surely the movement of the heavenly spheres is never able to raise the mind to a level higher than the spheres. But he who puts them under examination seems already to have transcended them, to have come near to God Himself and the free decision of the will. It is as if he is not constrained by heavenly fate, but guided, now by the providence of God which is above the heavens, and now by the freedom of the mind. Furthermore, although any adverse and, as I might say, fatal action habitually proceeds from one contrary position of the stars to another, no one dares to assert that will itself and reason, resisting the assumed force of the stars, arise from the force of the stars; but rather we understand that they flow from providence and freedom itself, by whose grace[b] we have spoken against fate.

28th June, 1477.
Florence.

30

Multos habet servos, qui multis servit

He has many servants, who serves many

Marsilio Ficino to Bernardo Bembo[a] of Venice: greetings.

FEBO Capella, Francesco d'Este, and Panfilo, the physician,[1] are asking us for the works of our Plato, all of which we translated some time ago from Greek into Latin. If by chance you should discover these distinguished men anywhere, greet them for me, and say that the translations cannot be sent this month.

You see, Bernardo, with how great a freedom I treat you. For I seem to have given a command, I know not how. But you, my Bembo, are the cause; for to each you show yourself to be such a man, that he who does not make use of the greatest freedom and trust with you, certainly seems to be of all men the least free and the least trusting. When you are serving others most freely, then are you most their master. But when others seem most to have dominion over you, then do they most freely serve you. No mastery is lighter, more effective and less anxious than one of love. No service is more constant,[b] more pleasing and more fruitful than a free one.

1st August, 1477.

31

Amicitia inter homines, nisi afflante deo, conflari non potest

Friendship between men cannot be kindled unless God breathes upon it

Marsilio Ficino of Florence to Ermolao Barbaro of Venice: greetings.

I WROTE some days ago a letter briefly discussing true friendship,[1] which I addressed not to one of my friends especially, but without particular ascription to all friends equally. A little later, most Latin Barbaro,[2] your fine letter was delivered to me, which catches me with the true bait of love, that is, with love itself, and calls the captive to love; and to love in such a way that you yourself, being one, now have what was to have been for many. For our discussion on true friendship, intended a moment ago[a] for the welfare of all my friends, you have suddenly claimed for yourself in particular. So that what was to have been addressed to all, is addressed to Ermolao alone. Therefore, just as previously, whilst writing[b] to all, I was led to write to the one above all so, after this, in loving all my friends, this one I will love above all.[c]

32

Marsilio Ficino to his fellow philosophers,[a] especially Ermolao Barbaro: greetings.[1]

ALL men, by common consent, define friendship as a kind[b] of union. Now since there cannot be union except with one, it seems right to inquire what that one is to which two, aspiring with one accord, become friends and are known as friends.

Are those who hold the same opinions necessarily friends? Not at all. For we may hold the same opinion on a great many things concerning both men and nature, and yet hate one another. So perhaps mutual goodwill consists not in opinion but in desire. Consider, should those who desire the same thing be called friends, at least as long as they so desire? No indeed! On the contrary, enmities are born from the very fact that we desire the same thing. Often those who covet the same treasure or official position or artistic honour grow jealous of one another,[c] become angry and quarrel. Perhaps someone may say that such discord arises between men because they desire some finite goods which one of them possesses but the other does not possess at all, or possesses unequally. But if men may be found who seek the same good, because[d] it is infinite, because it cannot anywhere be prevented from abounding without limit, then such men would not be agitated by any enmity among themselves. One might say that there is friendship amongst those who desire that same infinite good. But not even this seems to me sufficient for mutual goodwill, for by some natural instinct all men desire good of this kind, from this we all desire to be happy. Yet we do not all love one another.

Where then shall we find goodwill itself, which is nothing other than to will the good, unless we find it within the compass of that good itself which is all good, that is God? Certainly we shall not find it anywhere else.

Furthermore, as regards this subject, the human will can be moved towards God in two[e] principal ways. For it desires either to receive or to give. The first impulse is common and natural to everyone, since we all long for and seek from God as many things as possible, but in spite of this we neither love God nor men. The second impulse does not seem to exist equally in everyone. Certainly, very few are to be found who give up their very selves, and with themselves everything, to God; or rather, to speak more accurately, give all things back to God. For we are nothing, and we possess nothing, which we have not received from Him. Whoever gives his very self back to God, that is to say, he who turns to God the whole labour[f] and fruit of thought, desire and action, he alone[g] loves God for the sake of God himself, and cherishes all else for God.

The bootless lover of the bodily form cherishes just a picture of a beautiful[h] body, for the very reason that it is only the form and substance of the body which he loves. In the same way the true and devout lover cherishes created things simply because they are images or shadows of God the Creator, whom he loves. And the closer their resemblance, the more he marvels and gives praise. But most akin to the divine mind are minds which are dedicated to God before all else. And so, such minds are straightway drawn by ardour and sweetness of love beyond telling,[i] towards both God and each other,[j] as they first freely give themselves back to Him, as to a father, and then give themselves up in utter joy to each other, as to brothers. All other so-called friendships between men are nothing but acts of plunder. True charity, as the Apostle Paul says, 'seeketh not its own' but the benefit of another.[2] Although we daily take great pride in the honourable names of friendship, yet for the most part, such is our nature that each of us considers no one other than himself. In truth, each does not yield himself to another, but rather takes pains to receive from him some pleasure or advantage relating either to outward things and the body or to the mind.

And so to sum up, I would say, only that man is to be called a true and lawful lover who understands that in all the good things which at every point are presented to him and please him, nothing truly pleases him but the divine good itself, from which and through which all things are good. Thus he loves himself in all, and cherishes all in himself, in such a way that he does not love himself, save in Him through whom he has that which makes him worthy of being loved. Indeed, he cares his utmost for all men, as created with him by the same father. But some he chooses before others, as being more like his father. With these he leads a heavenly life on earth and in heaven a life that is beyond the heavens. Among these alone there is true friendship, that is, true union[k] from one and in one God. For a true and abiding union of many cannot be accomplished except through the eternal unity itself. But that true and eternal unity is God Himself, who alone is true simplicity and boundless power. Therefore it appears that only these men can freely proclaim with the prophet, 'Behold how good and how pleasant it is for brethren to dwell together in unity.'[3.]

33

Fortuna neque benefacere potest malis, neque malefacere
bonis

Fortune can neither benefit the wicked nor harm the good

Marsilio Ficino to Antonio Ivani of Sarzana: greetings.

IF you see someone suffering from incurable physical illness, tormented by a variety of pains in different parts of the body, will you
envy him his dainty feasts, his throng of attendants, soft pillows,
robe of purple and gilded bedchamber? Of course you cannot,[a]
unless you too are sick; as sick in mind as he in body. But those
who are slave to pleasures or riches, the pursuit of fame or power,
are beset by incurable sickness of mind and by manifold suffering.
So whoever looks enviously at such people sees nothing. That is
why the most blind of all seem to me to be those who say[b] that
fortune is blind, because she benefits the wicked, for whom in truth
nothing is good, or because she harms the good, for whom finally
nothing is bad. For as a man is in himself, so for him is that which
he receives.

  Among men, only those who have been deprived of the eye of
reason do not see with what wondrous reason each and every part
of the universe is put in place and set in motion. Only those men,
I would say, seem[c] to be at the mercy of fortune and the greatest
injustice, who, when the precise ordering of things points to the
infinite power, wisdom and justice of the Author, still either believe
that unreasoning fortune is in command, or else complain of divine
governance as if it were less than just.[1]

34

Matrimonii laus

In praise of matrimony

Marsilio Ficino to Antonio Pelotti, poet and excellent friend: greetings.

I CANNOT but highly approve, my Pelotti, of the fact that you have long been applying your mind to matrimony. By matrimony, man, as if divine, continuously preserves the human race through succession.[1] As though in gratitude, he returns to nature what he has received on loan, often with[a] interest. Like a true and generous sculptor he carves in his offspring a living[b] image of himself. Moreover, it is only, or principally, through these means that he obtains loving companionship for life and faithful guardianship of his affairs. He also has a domestic republic, in the governing[c] of which he may exercise the powers of prudence and all the virtues. At the same time, he provides the greatest protection for his old age, which he may spend more serenely in the bosom of a beloved wife, or in the arms of sons or grandsons, or in the care of relatives[d] by marriage. Finally, a wife and family offer us sweet solace from our labours, or at least the strongest incentive towards moral philosophy: wherefore Socrates used to confess that he had learnt much more moral philosophy from his wives than natural philosophy from Anaxagoras or Archelaus.[2]

Who would deny that from the time man was created nothing has been ordained or established for him by God which is more important and more ancient than matrimony, and that it is numbered among the sacred mysteries and held in the highest regard among all peoples? The powerful have always respected it and the wise have not disdained it, having seen that it is conducive to the ordering of society and does not hinder learning, provided one lives temperately and spends one's time carefully.

Although in youth our Plato rather neglected matrimony, yet finally in old age, moved by repentance, he made sacrifices to the Goddess of Nature, thereby to absolve himself publicly from the charges, first, of having ignored matrimony and, second, of being barren.[3] And he proclaimed in his *Laws* that a man who did not take a wife ought to be kept well away from all public duties and offices, and at the same time be burdened with public taxes more heavily than other citizens.[4] Hermes Trismegistus says that men of this sort are judged to be wholly unfruitful by human law, and like dry and barren trees by divine law.[5]

Under divine law only two kinds of men seem to be exempted: those who are quite unsuited to matrimony on account of some disability in their nature, or those who have devoted themselves to Minerva alone, as though they had pledged themselves to a wife. Nature herself excuses the former, while chaste Minerva would perhaps reproach her devotees if they were to pursue Venus.

Nature, which brought forth our Pelotti strong and handsome, would certainly have disapproved had he by chance neglected matrimony. And if Minerva, whom he has long served, tries to reprove him for mixing Venus with the Muses, Apollo and Mercury will come at once to his defence. They will surely say that Pelotti has dedicated to the sacred[e] Muses more and better songs after his wedding than before it. Finally, these sublime beings will bid one raise[f] one's eyes to the stars. There Phoebus, lord of the Muses, and their companion Mercury, move as escorts on either side of Venus, mother of love and of music, and walk with her almost[g] step for step, so to speak, and never go far from her.

But let us now leave the stars and return to mankind. I see you in the future, Antonio, frequently declaring in the following manner, within your own household, the benefits of taking a wife: 'Man alone, or man most of all, is a social being, as the philosophers say,[6] and for this reason the power of speech and of formulating laws is bestowed by nature on him alone. One who has lived alone may see himself as somewhat greater than man, but more probably as something less, since he who transcends[h] human powers while amongst men is rarer than the phoenix. He will play his part better than the rest of mankind if he has entered into a permanent and indissoluble family union. In this fellowship let him strive to serve and to learn how to guide the society[i] of mankind itself.

'Surely, just as the state consists of households, so skill in state affairs consists of the judicious handling of family affairs. He who has not learnt to govern his household will never know how to rule

the state. He will never love his country while he believes that its
blessings and its woes hardly apply to him. He will not care to instil
more serious conduct in himself who, by living alone, does not
provide a model of good conduct to a family. Anyone who is not
occupied[j] in family matters will each day become more neglectful
and degenerate through idleness and licence. He will never know
how to love anyone truly and steadfastly if he does not experience
the true and imperishable love of wife[k] and children. He will never
learn to endure the world, and by enduring to conquer, if he has
not had a family to teach him patience. He will not learn to feel
compassion for men if he has never experienced a weeping wife or
child, for indeed, if the mind is not unacquainted with misfortune,
it learns how to succour the afflicted.[7] But worst of all is the man[l]
who does not know how to watch over his family, nor that God
should frequently be invoked for their welfare. For the most part he
ignores the laws of mankind, men themselves, and the worship of
God. In short, it will be exceedingly difficult to avoid stripping man
bare, unless we clothe him with the lawful mantle of matrimony.

'Wherefore, friends, if you wish to be men and lawful sons of
God, increase the human race legitimately, and, just as you are like
God, so in the fashion of God, beget sons like yourselves. Nourish
them, rule them, direct them. And remember! In family affairs,
which need to be so carefully directed, have due regard to yourselves: gain skill and acquire authority in the earthly commonwealth;
be worthy of office in the heavenly[m] commonwealth.'

35

Philosophia sapientiam[a] gignit, sapientia parit felicitatem

Philosophy gives birth to wisdom, wisdom begets happiness

Marsilio Ficino to Sebastiano Salvini, his[b] cousin: greetings.

WHEN mighty and bountiful Juno[1] does not heed us, before blaming the Fates we should experience that divine power which, because it lives everywhere, is present in abundance for all who would be in its presence. It hears a man before he calls, gives heed to him who asks rightly. Therefore, Salvini, we should seek all our help from Minerva, so that one day we may raise ourselves from earth and ascend to the upper world.[2] Without doubt, the only power which can raise man up to the celestial head of the universe is that which was born from the head of supreme Jove[3] himself. But since it hearkens to no one except he ask rightly, let us strive our utmost, friend, to seek help from this source in the right way.

Now, who rightly entreats wisdom but he who does so wisely? But only he entreats wisdom wisely who from wisdom demands wisdom. We cannot seek anything wisely, either from her or from another, except through her; we cannot[c] wisely seek anything from her except herself. This has been taught us by Socrates who was, in the judgement[d] of Apollo, the wisest of all men.[4] As Plato recounts in *Phaedrus*, in his daily prayers the one thing he greatly desired from God was wisdom.[5] For that divine[e] man knew that for the unwise those things which commonly seem to be good are bad, whereas for the wise man, the things which are said to be bad, prove in the end to be good.

Happy is the man for whom all things end well: but they do so only for him[f] who uses them well. He alone uses each thing well who has learned of his own power and that of others, from wisdom. Therefore only the priests of wisdom are happy, for even in this condition of human wretchedness (if I may call it so) they are in bliss. But the rest are unfortunate, so much so that even in human happiness they are wretched.

From this the great worth and divinity of the lawful philosophy become apparent; for on this the perfect priesthood of wisdom most surely takes its stand. Yet it is treated so unworthily and with so little respect by the great mass of people that those who alone[g] are really wise, and through whom the rest have the means to be wise[h] about anything, are considered more foolish than anyone else. Furthermore, these men are thought to conceive God ill by those who have learnt from the philosophers how to worship God; for it is from the reasonings of the philosophers that they understand that that God whom they worship exists.

How very false is the judgment of the crowd! Once the crowd thought the philosopher Democritus to be a fool, when, having become truly wise, he began to mock the folly of mortals and was judged by the most wise physician Hippocrates to be the most discerning of all men.[6] Then they condemned the divine Socrates[i] for holding an apparently corrupt view of the gods;[7] yet because his view of God was more direct than that of others, he was called by that very god of theirs the wisest man of all.

But let the foolish crowd laugh as much as it likes. Let it mock philosophers as being foolish and wicked. Meanwhile, may philosophers mourn with Heraclitus the crowd's pathetic laughter, and with Democritus laugh at its ridiculous tears.[8]

36

Non est sanus, cui salubria displicent

The man who is displeased by health-giving things is not healthy

Marsilio Ficino to Jacopo Bracciolini,[1] son of the orator Poggio and heir to his father's art: greetings.

RECENTLY, when reading a philosophic letter, 'From Plutarch the Platonist to the Emperor Trajan', Bracciolini suddenly came to mind, for I know that whatever is best gives him great pleasure. Now Plutarch gives me the greatest pleasure, because he praises nothing that is not good and there is nothing good which he does not praise to the full. According to physicians, there is no surer sign of healthy taste than for that which is health-giving to seem delectable and, conversely, for that which is harmful to be distasteful.

But now hear this philosophic letter to an emperor which is in fact the preface, addressed to the Emperor Trajan, to Plutarch's book *On the Government of State and Empire*. This is a book which Policrates[2] translated almost word for word.

'Plutarch to Trajan: greetings.

'I have recognised your modesty in not grasping for the highest office, which nonetheless you have always striven to merit by fine conduct.[a] The further you are seen to be from the charge of ambition, the more worthy are you deemed.[b] So I rejoice in your virtue, and also in my fortune, provided you govern rightly what you have well earned. Otherwise, I have no doubt that you will be thrown into danger, and I be the subject of abusive tongues. For Rome does not condone weakness in her emperors, and public opinion usually flings the transgressions of disciples back at their teachers. Thus Seneca is reviled by the tongues of his detractors for the crimes of his pupil Nero;[3] the temerity of his young men is laid at Quintilian's door;[4] and Socrates is blamed for having been too indulgent[c] with his ward.[5]

'But whatever you undertake will be right if you do not depart from yourself. If you first compose yourself and then dispose all things with virtue as your aim, all things, as one whole, will go well for you.

'I have represented to you the essence of political order and practice. If you are conforming to this, you have Plutarch as your authority on how to live. Otherwise, I call upon the letter before us to witness that you are not pursuing the ruin of government on Plutarch's authority.'

Farewell.

37

Marsilii Ficini florentini disputatio contra iudicium
astrologorum

*A disputation against the pronouncements of the
astrologers by Marsilio Ficino of Florence*

Marsilio Ficino to Francesco Ippoliti,[a] the distinguished Count of
Gazzoldo: greetings.

I HAVE written a book opposing the empty pronouncements of the
astrologers.[1] I am sending you the preface, and will send the rest as
soon as[b] our scribe has copied it.

These astrologers, in declaring that every single thing is necessarily brought to pass by the stars, are themselves involved in three
highly pernicious errors, and they involve the public in them too.
For insofar as they are able, they take away from God, Almighty
and Supreme, his own providence and his absolute sovereignty over
the universe. Next, they deny the justice of the angels; for according
to them, the angels move the celestial bodies in such a way that
from thence come forth all the crimes of men, all evil events for
good men, and all good events for evil men. Lastly, they take away
from men their free will and deprive them of all peace of mind, for
it seems to the astrologers that men, no less than beasts, are driven
hither and thither.[c]

If they predict good events, which they usually do infrequently,[d]
uneasily and in complete obscurity, they commonly envelop them
in the greatest difficulties, whence it happens that we benefit very
little. But if, very occasionally, they foretell[e] that these events will
happen without great exertion, we are thereby rendered idle, arro-
gant and careless. And if by some chance it turns out as they have
foretold, the long-awaited pleasure proves after all to be not so
pleasing. If, however, they threaten evils, which happens much
more often, either we long anticipate events that will come much
later, or we miserably[f] imagine things that will never come, and by
imagining suffer.[2]

Then if the Fates cannot be avoided, they are foreseen and foretold to no purpose. Yet if they can be avoided by some method, the inevitability of fate is falsely maintained by the astrologers. They will probably say, I suppose, that this also is in the Fates, that once in a while one thing out of many may be foreknown and guarded against. Thus it follows that among the Fates there will be contention, so that one will be determined to harm a man and another to protect him. However, let us, for the present, concede this to the astrologers, lest[g] perhaps we appear to anyone to be too stubborn. But we shall never concede that it also stands in the decrees of the Fates that many people should disbelieve them and many besides contradict them. For how does fate[h] now impel Marsilio to pit all his strength in fighting fate? He now inveighs against fate, certainly not with the strength of fate itself, but rather with the power of something contrary and even superior in virtue. For necessity can in no wise fight against her own self, thereby denying that necessity exists and annihilating herself at her own instigation, and by her own sting.

What then is the meaning of that common saying, 'We are moved by the Fates; believe in them'?[3] But if we consider the matter more carefully, we are moved not so much by the Fates themselves as by the foolish advocates of the Fates. Believe me, you will not yield to the Fates provided you do not believe these fools who veil in obscurity not the truth, as it is said the Sybil did, but falsehoods. Besides, they do not predict particular things for individuals, but things common to all.

These word-mongers bring so many things before the public that it is no wonder if among the multitude of lies they occasionally stumble by chance on something[i] true! They want to be wise for others since they know so little for themselves.

It is worth reflecting on how destitute they are, how mean, how unfortunate in their business dealings, how inept and imprudent in their affairs. If perchance they engage in commerce, they have much less foresight regarding the turn of the market than other merchants; if in medicine, their foreknowledge[j] of the course and outcome of an illness is much less than that of other physicians, and their care of the body is worst of all. And although they profess divination, yet[k] they appear to live and die according to chance.

So pray arise, philosophers. Arise all who yearn for freedom and most precious[l] peace. Come,[m] gird yourselves now with the shield and spear of Pallas. War is impending for us against those petty ogres. By foreknowledge of the future they presume to equate themselves with God, who is infinite.[n] By upholding heavenly fate, they presume to take away freedom of direction from God, who is above the heavens, and who is the highest freedom. But those who aspire with such arrogance to climb to the world of the gods will in humiliation be cast down headlong to the infernal regions.

Almighty God, extend your hand to us from on high. Give your soldiers strength; for now we are undertaking to defend your sovereignty.[o] Hasten to our aid, O divine powers who revolve the heavenly spheres; help us as we defend your justice against the wicked enemies, who accuse you of extreme injustice. You too, O human race! Give us your unprejudiced support, for it is your most precious freedom and peace, the freedom and peace of all men, that we are protecting. So may we triumph over the diviners, albeit not divine but mightily profane, who have for so long been shackling us[p] to their illusions; so at last may we be able freely to exclaim, 'Wickedness is once more trampled underfoot, and victory elevates us to the heavenly kingdom.'[4] [q]

38

Prohemium Marsilii Ficini in opusculum eius de Vita Platonis, ad Franciscum Bandinum

The preface of Marsilio Ficino to his short work on the life of Plato, addressed to[a] *Francesco Bandini*

THERE was recently born to me, O magnanimous Bandini, on the birthday[b] of the omnipotent Christ, a certain Plato.[1] Although far from equal to that Plato who was his forefather and our father, he nevertheless seems in a strange way to be of similar nature. Turning to him, I said, 'O Plato, will you seek again your ancestral and native seat of Athens?' But he immediately exclaimed, 'O unjust fate! Alas, nowhere do I have an ancestral home! O iron age! in which brutal[c] Mars has laid in ruins the Attic citadels of Pallas.[2] Therefore, Marsilio, not into unhappy Greece, but into Hungary shall I go for refuge. For there flourishes the great King Matthias, who, sustained at once[d] by a wonderful power and wisdom in these years of manifest decline, will provide once more a sanctuary to the wise and powerful Pallas, that is, the philosophic schools of the Greeks. Further, my Bandini lives happily there at the court of that most fortunate King of Hungary.[3] It was Bandini who once[e] celebrated the birth of the divine Plato at his own expense and with regal splendour within the City of Florence, and was also amongst the first present when the same convivium was reinstated outside the City by the illustrious Medici.[4] Therefore, I shall now go swiftly and eagerly to these friends in Hungary.' Then I said to this Plato, 'It is an honour,[f] it is our honour; profit by this more favourable destiny.'[5]

39

Montes non separant[a] animos montibus altiores

Mountains do not separate spirits which are loftier than mountains

Marsilio Ficino of Florence to the Reverend Father in Christ, Nicolaus Bathory, the Lord Bishop of Vacz in Hungary: greetings.

WHEN I received your letters, and those of Bandini, in which you strongly urge me to set out for Hungary, which would greatly please Matthias, His Most Serene Highness the King of Hungary, I had already finished the five keys to Platonic Wisdom.[1] One of these, shorter than the others, is coming to you. But for me to come is difficult; and then, to live under that sky, perhaps more difficult.

In truth, to speak more accurately, if I were to come to you, I must needs leave you first, before I am able to return. But[b] it is not possible for me to leave those with whom long ago my soul was made one through the call of the Muse.

Continue, I pray, to love your Marsilio, who, on account of your outstanding virtues, ardently loves you. Likewise love our Francesco Bandini, a man outstanding in genius and magnanimity. Commend us both, if it is fitting, to the most fortunate King Matthias; in a short time something will be coming to him from our workshop which will commend us, as best it may. Farewell, and yet live with me, happy spirits, in spite of [c] the mountains which seem to separate us. Live with me, happy spirits, more lofty far than even the most lofty mountains. I am to you that which each one is to himself. You are to me that which my two eyes are to me.[2]

25th May, 1479.[3] [d]

FINIS

Notes on the Letters

ABBREVIATIONS

Diog. Laert.—Diogenes Laertius, *Lives of Eminent Philosophers*.
Kristeller, *Studies*—P. O. Kristeller, *Studies in Renaissance Thought and Letters*.
Letters—The Letters of Marsilio Ficino, Vol. 1, 1975, Vol. 2, 1978.
Marcel—R. Marcel, *Marsile Ficin*, Paris, 1958.
Opera—Marsilius Ficinus, *Opera Omnia*, Basle, 1576.
Pat. Lat.—J. P. Migne, *Patrologiae Latinae*, 2nd ed. 1878 seq.
Pat. Graec.—J. P. Migne, *Patrologiae Graecae*, 1857–1866.
Pliny, *Nat. Hist.*—Pliny, *Natural History*.
Sup. Fic.—P. O. Kristeller, *Supplementum Ficinianum*.

1

1 Written in the Spring of 1477: see letter 12 and note 1. This letter is one of eleven letters comprising the *Sermoni Morali della Stultitia et Miseria degli Uomini*, translated into Italian by Ficino in June 1478 and addressed to Jacopo Guicciardini. See *Sup. Fic.*, I, p. cxi.
2 Iamblichus, *Life of Pythagoras*, XXIV, 109; Porphyry, *Life of Pythagoras*, 42.

3

1 Cicero, *De Officiis*, III, xv, 62, after Ennius.

4

1 The preface to Ficino's translation of the Psalter (*Sup.Fic.*, II, p. 187) is almost identical with this letter up to the words *praeter amorem cultumque divinum* (except love and divine worship). The preface was apparently written after the letter. See Kristeller, *The Philosophy of Marsilio Ficino*, p. 316.
2 *Theriaca*, an antidote to poison, especially snake-bite.

5

1 Seneca, *De Beneficiis*, I, vi, 1–2; see also Seneca, *ibid*, I, ix, 1.
2 Ficino's *De Christiana Religione*.

8

1 Pace was secretary to the Archbishop of Florence, Rinaldo Orsini.
2 *Pace* means 'peace' in Italian.
3 Lorenzo de' Medici. Some metaphor is intended here: Phoebus represents song and music, and Jove is the 'heavenly father'. Lorenzo was a poet and Orsini was Archbishop of Florence.
4 *e.g.* Aristotle, *De Generatione et Corruptione*, II, i; *Physics* I, v-vi.
5 Written in 1478, according to Kristeller (*Sup. Fic.*, I, p. ic), since it is mentioned in a subsequent letter in Book V (*Opera*, p. 806,3) as having been written a few days before the wars of the Pazzi conspiracy. If the date is correct, this letter was written less than a fortnight before the Pazzi conspiracy (see Preface p. xi) which was immediately followed by war.

9

1 Written in the Spring of 1477: see letter 12 and note 1.
2 Ficino may be alluding to Dante's *Inferno*, Canto XIII, which describes the wood of suicides, whose souls have taken root in the ground to become gnarled trees, giving forth dark leaves, twisted branches, and poison instead of fruit.

10

1 Both letters are from Book II of the *Epistolae*, *Opera*, pp. 697, 717. An amended version of the text is given in Marcel, *Théologie Platonicienne*, vol III, pp. 347, 370.
2 *Imaginum* (shadow) in the Latin.
3 The light which blinded St. Paul, and his conversion, are described in Acts 9: 1-9.
4 A son of Phoebus who resolved to find his true origin. He requested his father that he be allowed to drive the chariot of the sun for one day, but he was inexperienced at guiding the chariot. The horses were plunged into confusion, and heaven and earth were threatened with universal conflagration. Jupiter struck the rider with a thunderbolt and hurled him down from heaven. Hyginus, *Fabulae*, CLII, CLIV.
5 The Emperor Flavius Claudius Julianus, sometimes called Julian the Apostate, who was brought up as a Christian but was later converted to Paganism. He was encouraged to believe that he had been chosen to restore the pagan religion and he composed an oration for the pagan festival of the sun, *natalis solis invicti*

(birthday of the invincible sun), held on 25th December as a pagan alternative to the celebration of Christ's birth.

6 Claudian, who lived in the reign of Theodosius, was the last notable Latin poet of the classical tradition. He wrote an unfinished epic *De Raptu Proserpinae* (The Rape of Persephone). Persephone was carried off by Pluto to the underworld. Phoebus and Persephone were both offspring of Zeus.

7 St. Luke, physician and constant companion of St. Paul. See Colossians 414. Hierotheus is mentioned several times by Pseudo–Dionysius in *The Divine Names*, and is referred to as his teacher.

8 Paul of Tarsus (St. Paul) is figuratively referred to as Aesculapius, the Latin form of the Greek Asklepios, physician and a god of healing.

9 According to Plato, both Homer and Stesichorus were blinded because they sang profanely about love and so offended the deity. See Plato, *Phaedrus*, 243 AB.

10 Numenius of Apamea (2nd century AD) wrote extensively on the teachings of Plato and Pythagoras and the occult meaning of Greek mythology. For this anecdote see Macrobius, *Commentary on the Dream of Scipio*, I, ii, 19 (ed. Stahl, p. 87). The Eleusinian goddesses appeared to Numenius in a dream dressed as courtesans to show him how, by his writings, he had prostituted them to every passer-by.

11 Pherecydes of Syros (*c.* 550 BC), a Pythagorean who wrote a work on cosmogony. He was one of the first to write on the doctrine of the immortality of the soul. Diog. Laert., I,116–122; Cicero, *Tusculanos*, I, xvi, 38.

12 'Hipparchus, being guilty of writing the tenets of Pythagoras in plain language, was expelled from the school and a pillar raised to him as if he were dead.' See Clement of Alexandria, *Stromata*, V, ix (*Pat. Graec.*, 9); Iamblichus, *Life of Pythagoras*, XVII, 75. The 'sacred seer' is Pythagoras.

13 The reference is to Dionysius II, tyrant of Sicily, who tried to use Plato's philosophy for his own ends. See Plato, *Epistles*, III, VII.

14 Apollonian: the hidden meaning of Plato's philosophy; Apollo was the god of prophecy and oracles.

15 Ficino seems to be alluding to Matthew 7:6 (Vulgate). *Cf.* Matthew 15:26, Mark 7:27.

16 The Latin word is *Davus*, a common name for slaves in classical times. Ficino may be thinking of a passage in Terence's *Andros*, I, ii, 24: '*Davus sum, non Oedipus.*'

17 The disciple who restored Saul's sight. Acts 9:10–18.

18 Lorenzo de' Medici was born on the 1st January (1449).

12

1 The following are the six short works which Ficino sent to Marco Aurelio with this letter:
  1 'In praise of philosophy' (letter 13).
  2 'In praise of medicine' (letter 14).

3. 'Nothing is more shameful than a man in whose house all things are more beautiful before the soul' (Vol. 2, letter 60).
4. 'In order to change your lot for the better, change the form of your soul for the better' (letter 9).
5. 'All the good things of the world are evil for the man who leads a corrupt life in the world' (Vol. 2, letter 40).
6. 'No one can be envied, who can see how many times we all are driven both inwardly and outwardly by the Furies' (letter 1).

It is worth remarking that 3, 4 and 5 above are addressed to Mankind.
See also letter 14 note 22 and Notes on the Latin Text, note k at the end of letter 14.

13

1 This speech is an early work of Ficino, written probably when he was a student. See Kristeller, *Sup. Fic.*, I, p.c and letter 12, note 1.
2 Compare this with a passage in Augustine, *City of God*, VIII, 9 (tr. H. Bettenson p. 311): 'There are philosophers who have conceived of God, the supreme and true God, as the author of all created things, the light of knowledge, the final good of all activity, and who have recognized him as being for us the origin of existence, the truth of doctrine and the happiness of life. They may be called most suitably Platonists.' Augustine would seem to be Ficino's main source for this idea.
3 This idea does not appear to occur in the three dialogues mentioned, but see Plato, *Philebus*, 65: 'If we are not able to hunt the good with one idea only, with three we may catch our prey; beauty, symmetry, truth are the three . . .'
4 *Cf.* Iamblichus, *On the Egyptian Mysteries*, VIII, 2–3 (paras. 261–3); I,5 (18): existence, power, activity (See also Ficino's epitome of Iamblichus' *De Mysteriis, Opera*, p. 1873). *Cf.* Proclus, *Elements of Theology*, 101–3 *seq.*: being, life, intelligence.
5 Dionysius the Areopagite (Pseudo-Dionysius), *The Divine Names*, V: on Deity as existence, life and wisdom. See also Ficino's commentary to the *Mystical Theology* of Dionysius, *Opera*, p. 1013.
6 Hilary (300–367 AD), Bishop of Poitiers, who was a convert from Neoplatonism wrote a work on the Trinity, *De Trinitate* (*Pat. Lat.*, 10).
7 *De Vera Religione*, LV, 112 (*Pat.Lat.*, 34); *City of God*, VIII, 5.
8 The three divisions of philosophy: natural, rational and moral, corresponding to the threefold conception of God as the cause of existence, the principle of reason and the rule of life: Augustine, *City of God*, VIII, 4. See also chs. 6–8.
9 Hermes Trismegistus, *Pimander*, X, 6.
10 Pythagoras, *Golden Verses*, XXXVI (final verses). See Ficino, *Opera*, p. 1979.
11 Plato, *Republic*, VII, 540.
12 See Plotinus, *Enneads*, IV, 7, 10, on the immortality of the soul, (Mckenna, p. 354), which also quotes a line from Empedocles describing the soul that has ascended to the pure intellect: 'Farewell: I am to you an immortal God.' (Diels, *Frag. der Vorsok.*, 31, B112).

13 For this quotation see Pseudo-Apuleius, *De Mundo*, proem. The Greek original (Περι Κόσμου) is by an unknown Platonic writer of the 1st century AD, not by Aristotle.

14 See Plato, *Statesman*, 271D–272A for a description of the age of Cronos or the Golden Age; see Plato *Republic*, V, 473D for the belief that the ills of the human race will end only when power and wisdom are united in the same man.

15 Pythagoras, *Golden Verses*, XXXVI (final verses). See Ficino *Opera*, p. 1979.

14

1 This speech was apparently written when Ficino was studying medicine at Bologna University (1458–9). Marcel (pp. 239–40) dates it between 1459–1462, but Kristeller (*Studies* p. 195) believes that no certain date can be ascribed to its composition. Medicine and law were frequently praised in the writings of humanists; see for example Coluccio Salutati, *De Nobilitate Legum et Medicinae*, ed. Garin (Florence 1947). Compare this early work of Ficino's with a letter on the nobility of medicine written *c.* 1474 (*Opera* p. 645; *Letters*, Vol. 1, letter 81).

2 See Ficino, *Theologia Platonica*, V, 5, (ed. Marcel, Vol. I, p. 181). 'The source of man is the universal nature of man; the end of man is happiness; his substance is the body, his form the soul.' (*Efficiens hominis causa est natura universalis et homo; finis humana felicitas; materia corpus; forma est anima*).

3 Sons of Aesculapius and famous physicians in the Trojan war. After death they received divine honours and temples were built to them. Homer, *Iliad*, IV, 193 *seq.*

4 See Ficino's epitome to Iamblichus, *De Mysteriis*, *Opera*, p. 1883; 'In the temple of Apollo dreams are experienced which cure diseases, and even the art of medicine itself has arisen through sacred dreams.' (*Sic in aesculapii templo accipiuntur, quibus morbi curantur, ipsaque ars medendi somniis est comparata divinis.*) An account of the origin of medicine is also given in Pliny (*Nat. Hist.*, XXIX, ii), where Hippocrates is said to have written down the remedies found inscribed on the walls of the temple of Aesculapius at Cos by patients who had recovered after applying such remedies.

5 Most of these names are mentioned in Celsus, *De Medicina*, (proem, 1–12) and in Pliny's *Natural History* in connection with various remedies. The following alternatives in spelling should be noted: Diocles Caristius for Diocles of Carystus; Erophylus for Herophilus; Glaucias for Glacias; Themison for Chemison; Pleistonicus for Plistonicus. A number of physicians of the name of Apollonius are mentioned by Celsus.

Pythagoras and several of his followers were physicians and his school appears to have exercised a considerable influence on the subsequent development of the art. Diocles of Carystus (4th century BC) belonged to the Dogmatic school of medicine.

Herophilus (335–280 BC) and Erasistratus (*d.* 280 BC) belong to the Alexandrian school of medicine, which continued the traditions of Hippocrates and his school, surpassing them in the study of anatomy. Fragments of their lost works are quoted by Galen and Celsus. Plistonicus was a pupil of Praxagoras and wrote on anatomy.

Serapion and Glacias of Tarentum are named as the founders of the Empiric school of Alexandria. They based their whole practice upon experience. Chemison was a pupil of the Greek physician Asclepiades of Bithynia and he founded a new system of medicine.

Galen (130 AD) gathered the divergent threads of ancient medicine into a comprehensive system, out of which the greater part of modern medicine has flowed. He restored medicine to a state of unity it had not enjoyed since the time of Hippocrates. His method was to reduce all knowledge acquired by the observation of facts to general principles. His writings were translated into Arabic in the 9th century and it was chiefly through Arab medical writers that his system found its way back to western Europe in the Middle Ages. His works were first printed in a Latin translation in Venice, 1490.

6 Homer, *Odyssey*, IV, 231.

7 Plato, *Timaeus*, 24.

8 Diog. Laert., I, 2 (Prologue) mentions the names of five Magi: Ostanas, Astrampsychos, Gobryas, Pazatas and Zoroaster, corresponding with the first five mentioned by Ficino; Apuleius, *Apology*, 90, gives six further names: Carinondas, Damigeron, Moses, Jannes, Apollobex and Dardanus. Ficino perhaps used a corrupt text; the text should have read *sim carmendas . . . his Moses . . .* not *sinicariondas . . . Hismoses*. (See Marcel, *op. cit.,* p. 608). See Pliny on the Magi; 'The art of medicine and magic flourished together in the time of Hippocrates.' (*Plenumque miraculi et hoc, pariter utrasque artes effloruisse medicinam dico magicenque, eadem aetate illam Hippocrate.*) Apollobex the Copt and Dardanus the Phoenician are mentioned; Jannes is described as an Egyptian Magician. Pliny, *Nat. Hist.*, XXX, 1(2) *et seq.* (Loeb ed., Vol. VIII, p. 285).

9 Pliny, *Nat. Hist.*, VII, xxiv, 88.

10 Avicenna (Ibn Sina, 980–1037 AD) wrote on philosophy as well as medicine and became even more celebrated than Hippocrates or Galen. His most famous work, the *Canon of Medicine*, is an encyclopaedia of medical knowledge based upon Galen and Aristotle.

11 Two writers on medicine bear the name Serapion: Serapion the Elder (Yahya ibn Sarafyun, 9th century) whose work, the *Practica sive breviarium*, was first printed in Venice in 1479; and Serapion the Younger (Ibn Sarabi), an Arab physician of the 12th century who wrote the *Liber de Simplici Medicina*, 1st edition, Milan, 1473.

Johannes or Johannitius (Hunayn bin Ishaq al Ibadi), translator and commentator of Hippocrates and Galen and Johannes Mesue (Yuhanna bin Masawayh) both belonged to the school of Baghdad (9th century). Another writer, Mesue the Younger of Damascus (11th century), wrote *De Simplicibus* which became a standard work on medicine.

Avenzoar (Ibn Zuhr) wrote a work on the diagnosis and treatment of diseases. Abumeron (Abu Merwan Abd al-Malik, 12th century) was a Moorish writer of Spain. His friend and pupil, Averroes of Cordova (Ibn Rushd), well-known for his philosophical writings, also wrote on medicine and was widely read in Latin.

Rhazes (Abu Bakr ar-Razi, 925 AD) was a Persian who practised at Baghdad. He wrote the *Liber ad Almansorem*, a reference work on medicine. Abugasis or Abulcasis (Abu al-Qusaim) of Cordova (11th century) wrote a medical encyclopaedia which was chiefly valued in the Middle Ages for its section on surgery. Isaac Israeli (*c*. 865–955) was a Jewish writer who combined neoplatonic ideas and natural science in his medical and philosophical works.

Hali (Ali bin Abbas al-Majusi), a Persian, wrote a medical text-book known as *The Royal Book*, which was translated into Latin.

Ficino may not have read all these writers individually. Many would be mentioned or quoted in the canons of learning available in the Middle Ages, such as Roger Bacon's *Opus Majus*.

12 Cornelius Celsus (1st century AD) wrote *De Medicina*, intended as a layman's manual and a general introduction to the history of medicine; it was rediscovered in 1426, and became a model for medical writers of the Renaissance.

Apuleius of Madaura has been wrongly credited with writing certain medical works, such as *Herbarius* and *De Remediis Salutaribus*. Their anonymous author is called 'Apuleius Platonicus'.

Quintus Serenus was the author of a medical textbook in verse, the *Liber Medicinalis* (3rd century AD), which was widely read in the Middle Ages. Columella's *De Re Rustica* (agriculture) and Pliny's *Natural History* also enjoyed immense popularity.

Lactantius, apart from his theological writings, wrote a work on the beauty and adaptability of the human body, *De Opificio Dei sive de Formatione Hominis* (*Pat. Lat., 7*).

13 Hermes Trismegistus, *Asclepius*, I, 6a and *Corpus Hermeticum* (see Ficino, *Opera*, p. 1837 *seq.*).

14 Psalms 8:6.

15 Hippocrates, *Works*, ed. Littré, Vol. IX, p. 343.

16 Plato, *Charmides*, 156–7.

17 *ibid*. 156c.

18 See Genesis, chs. 2, 3. According to apocryphal sources the sin of Adam was the cause of physical and spiritual death.

19 Celsus, *De Medicina*, proem, 6 *seq*.

20 Abel, *Orphica*, LXVII; 'Hymns of Orpheus', LXVII, in *Thomas Taylor, Selected Writings*, ed. K. Raine. p. 274:
'And men without thy all-sustaining ease,
Find nothing useful, nothing formed to please.'

21 Homer, *Iliad*, XI, 514. Quoted in Plato, *Statesman*, 297E.

22 At the end of letter 14 MSS G4 and R10 have an addition which is set out in the Notes on the Latin Text, note k. The translation is as follows:
'Four short speeches follow, one after another:
the first begins: "If some farmer were not only etc."
the second: "Today while I was enquiring within myself for the main etc."
the third: "Man, why have you for so long accused etc."

the fourth: "Pythagoras charged his disciples etc."
These four speeches are amongst the above.'

15

1 This is a reference to Buonincontri's poem on astronomy, *Atlante* (Atlas). See biographical notes.

16

1 Psalms 46:1.
2 Augustine, *Confessions*, VII, xi.

18

1 This essay, together with the *Life of Plato*, originally formed the introduction to Ficino's *Philebus Commentary*, which was written before 1474 (according to Corsi before 1469) and delivered in a series of public lectures, possibly in the former church of Santa Maria degli Angeli in Florence, prefaced with these words: 'Since we are going to interpret the sacred philosophy of the divine Plato in this renowned place at the request of the leading citizens, I thought it appropriate that we should first briefly consider what philosophy is.' In 1477 the essay was added to the fourth book of letters (see *Sup. Fic.*, I, pp. c–ci). The original version is preserved in MS Vat. Lat. 5953; see *Sup. Fic.*, I, pp. 30–31 for variants.
2 See *Letters*, Vol. I, letter 123.
3 See letter 13.
4 See Augustine, *City of God*, VIII, 2, (tr. Bettenson, p. 299): 'Pythagoras . . . is credited with the coinage of the actual name of philosophy.'
5 Plato, *Republic*, VI, 485 *seq.* The passage which follows, down to 'greatest crimes' (in the Latin from *quicunque philosophus* to *a Platone dicuntur*) agrees in part with Ficino's epitome of Alcinous, *De Doctrina Platonis*, ch. 1 (*Opera*, p. 1946).
6 Plato, *Republic*, VI, 495.
7 On the importance of mathematics, see Plato, *Republic*, VII, 522 *seq.*
8 Plato, *Phaedo*, 67.
9 Plato, *Phaedrus*, 249C; *Theaetetus*, 176.
10 See Plato, *Republic*, VII, 526–31 for the order of the studies. The Latin word used by Ficino here is *Stereometria* (Solid Geometry). The Greek στερεομετρια is used to describe three-dimensional forms in Plato (*Epinomis*, 990D, but see note 33 to letter 19) and in Aristotle. Plato also uses στερεομετρια to designate cubic numbers (*Theaetetus*, 148B).
11 For the hymn on dialectic see Plato, *Republic*, VII, 532–4: 'When a person starts on the discovery of the absolute . . .'
12 Plato, *Timaeus*, 47B.

13 Plato, *Republic*, V, 473D; *Laws*, 713: 'There is said to have been in the time of Cronos a blessed rule and life, of which the best ordered of existing states is a copy.'

14 Hesiod, *Works and Days*, 120 *seq.*

19

1 An earlier version of this *Life of Plato* originally formed the first chapter of Ficino's *Philebus Commentary*, and was written between 1469 and 1474. It is preserved in MS Vat. Lat. 5953 (See Kristeller, *Sup. Fic.*, I, pp. 30–1). This MS has the sigla V10. This final version was written at the end of 1477, and in a number of MSS (L. 12, L0 1, *etc.*) it forms an introduction to the dialogues of Plato translated into Latin by Ficino. Contemporary with this *Life of Plato* is one by Guarino Veronese (Vat. Lat. 8086).
Ficino's life of Plato is drawn mainly from Diogenes Laertius, *Lives of Eminent Philosophers* (3rd century AD). A medieval version of this work – *De Vita et Moribus Philosophorum* by Walter Burley is found in Vat. Lat. 3081. A large number of other sources are also used, notably Apuleius, Cicero, Plutarch and the *Epistles* and *Dialogues* of Plato. The earliest extant life of Plato is Apuleius' *De Platone et eius Dogmate* (*Concerning Plato and his Teachings*—2nd century AD). Plato's disciples Speusippus, Aristotle and Xenocrates all wrote accounts of his life which have been lost. Olympiodorus of Alexandria (6th century AD) wrote a *Life of Plato* which is extant. Many of the anecdotes mentioned by Ficino are outside the mainstream tradition of Plato's life. For more detailed information on the sources, see Alice S. Riginos, *Platonica, The Anecdotes Concerning the Life and Writings of Plato*, Leiden, 1976. A forthcoming study by Alice Riginos will deal with the sources of Ficino's *De Vita Platonis*.

2 Diog. Laert., III, 1 (Life of Plato). The same story of Plato's divine birth is given in Apuleius, *De Platone et eius Dogmate*, I, 1 and Olympiodorus, *Life of Plato*, I. A similar story concerning the birth of Pythagoras is given in Iamblichus, *Life of Pythagoras*, II, 4–5, who was said to be descended from Apollo.

3 John of Salisbury, *Policraticus*, VII, v. The legend of Plato's divine birth from Apollo is justified by Plutarch on the grounds that Plato was the healer of men's souls as Apollo was the healer of their bodies. Plato came to be permanently associated with the divine physician Asclepius: Plutarch, *Quaestionum Convivialium* (Table Talk), 8,1: *Moralia* IX. Plato was also associated with Apollo by the fact that the Academy celebrated his birthday on the seventh day of the month of Thargelion, Apollo's birthday. Thargelion corresponds roughly with May. Julius Firmicus's horoscope quoted below, however, would place his birthday in January or February.

4 Apuleius, *op. cit.*, 1, states that Plato was born the day after Socrates' birthday. This would make Plato's birthday the seventh day of Thargelion of the first year of the eighty-eighth Olympiad, *i.e.* 427 BC.

5 Ficino is possibly referring to the first version of *De Amore*, written between 1467 and 1469 which is not extant. The second version does not contain this description. See *Sup. Fic.*, I, p. cxxv.

6 Julius Firmicus Maternus, *Matheseos*, VI, 30, 24. Ficino has paraphrased the original words. 'If the ascendant is in Aquarius, and Mars, Mercury and Venus are in conjunction in that degree; Jupiter is on the descendant in Leo; the sun is on the anafora of the ascendant in Pisces; the moon is in the fifth house in Gemini, in trine to the ascendant; and Saturn is in the ninth house in Libra— this chart produces an interpreter of divine and celestial matters. He possesses a combination of learned speech and divine intelligence and is trained by some kind of heavenly power to give true expression to all secrets of divinity. This chart is said to have been that of Plato.' (J. F. Maternus, *Matheseos, Ancient Astrology, Theory and Practice* p. 209, tr. Jean Rhys Bram, Noyes Classical Studies, Park Ridge, N. J., 1975).

7 Cicero, *De Divinatione*, I, xxxvi. A longer version of this story is recounted in Olympiodorus, *Life of Plato*, I, where the event takes place in the hills of Hymettus whilst a sacrifice is being made to Apollo and the gods by Plato's parents on his behalf (see *Prolegomena to Platonic Philosophy*, I, 2, ed. Westerink, Amsterdam, 1962).

8 Diog. Laert., III, 5; Apuleius, *De Platone et eius Dogmate*, I, 1, the longer version of the story. The swan was a bird sacred to Apollo.

9 Diog. Laert., III, 5; Ficino also admitted burning some of his early compositions on pleasure (*Opera*, p. 933,3, letter to Martinus Uranius).

10 Academia (Ἑκαδημεια) was a piece of land near Athens, originally belonging to the hero Hecademus that Plato purchased for his school, from which the word 'academy' derives. *Cf.* Diog. Laert., III, 8.

11 Basil, *Sermones, De Legendis Libris Gentilium*, 7, (*Pat. Graec.*, 31). Jerome, *Adversus Jovinianum*, II, 9 (*Pat. Lat.* 23).

12 Diog. Laert., III, 4. A pun on the word πλατων (platon), which in Greek means 'broad'.

13 Diog. Laert., III, 8; III, 18–21. Diogenes Laertius, on whom Ficino relies at this point, would appear to be inaccurate. The battle of Tanagra took place in 457 BC about thirty years before Plato was born. The battle at Delium took place in 424 BC when Plato would have been about four years old. It is possible that Diogenes has mistaken the presence of Plato at this battle for that of Socrates. The latter certainly fought there. It is uncertain to which campaign at Corinth Diogenes is referring, but none is known at which Plato could have been present. Diogenes gives as his source Aristoxenus, who wrote, *inter alia*, many biographies, now lost, amongst which was one of Plato.

14 Helice in Achaia in the Bay of Corinth was overwhelmed by a tidal wave in the great earthquake of 372 BC: Pliny, *Nat. Hist.*, II, 92.

15 Diog. Laert., III, 21–2; see Plato, *Epistles*, VII, 327–333, and Plutarch's *Life of Dion* for an account of Plato's friendship with Dion and his voyages to Sicily.

16 Diog. Laert., III, 23; Plutarch, *Life of Dion*, XVIII–XX; Plato, *Epistles*, VII, 338 *seq.*

17 Pliny, *Nat. Hist.*, VII, xxx, (110).

18 Diog. Laert., III, 23. Aelian, *Varia Historia*, II, 41. Plato also declined a similar invitation from the Cyrenaeans because they were so prosperous; Plutarch, *Ad Principem Ineruditum*, 779 (*Moralia*, X). *Cf.* Plato, *Epistles*, VII, 330D–331D for

the idea that a philosopher should only give advice where there is a reasonable likelihood that it will be heeded. He may never use force to bring about a change in a constitution.

19 See Plato, *Epistles*, III, 316A, where Plato is described as having worked on the preamble to the laws of the Syracusans.

20 For this group of Plato's followers who were described as lawgivers, see Plutarch, *Adversus Colotem*, XXXII (*Moralia*, XIV).

21 Augustine, *De Vera Religione*, III, 5 (*Pat. Lat.*, 34).

22 Diog. Laert., III, 26.

23 Seneca, *De Ira*, II, xxi, 10; *ibid*, III, xii, 6.

24 Diog. Laert., III, 39.

25 See Plato, *Epistles*, VII, 326B for a reference to Syracusan banquets, with men eating twice a day and never sleeping alone.

26 See especially Ficino, *De Amore*, VII, ii, 'Socrates the true lover', and xvi (ed. Marcel pp. 242–5, 260–2).

27 Diog. Laert., III, 40. *Cf.* Plato, *Epistles*, II, 311, on the great importance which men of superior virtue attach to the memorial of themselves to be left after their death, in the minds of men.

28 Aristotle, *Problemata*, XXX, 953a; quoted by Cicero, *Tusculanos*, I, xxxiii, 80.

29 Diog. Laert., IV, 6 (Life of Xenocrates); Plutarch, *Life of Dion*, XVII, 1.

30 Diog. Laert., III, 46.

31 The Greek text of Diogenes gives 'Chamaeleon *adds* Lycurgus . . .' Chamaeleon was a peripatetic writer of the 3rd century BC, not a member of Plato's Academy. Mnesistratus is mentioned only by Diogenes as an authority for the statement that Demosthenes was Plato's pupil. See Diog. Laert., III, 47.

32 This is Ficino's interpretation.

33 See Diog. Laert., III, 57–60. *Ion* is missing from this list, although it was translated into Latin by Ficino. The following works, once attributed to Plato, are now considered to be spurious: *Axiochus, De Justo, De Virtute, Demodocus, Sisyphus, Eryxias, Epinomis, Hipparchus, Amatores, Theages, Minos* and the *Definitions*. The following works are of dubious authenticity: *Alcibiades* 1 & 2, *Hippias Maior & Minor, Menexenus* and *Cleitophon*.

Of the dialogues now regarded as spurious, Ficino translated *Epinomis, Hipparchus, Amatores, Minos, Theages* and *Cleitophon*. Of these only the last he considered was possibly not by Plato. Ficino also translated *Axiochus*, which he considered to be the lost dialogue on death by Xenocrates, and the *Definitions* which he attributed to Speusippus.

Of the *Epistles*, Seven and Eight are generally regarded as genuine, whilst One and Twelve are thought to be spurious. The authenticity of the rest is dubious. The only one questioned by Ficino was Thirteen, which he did not translate. See *Sup. Fic.*, I, cxlvii *seq.*

34 See note 33 above.

35 *Cf.* Diog. Laert., III, 49 for other classifications.

36 *Cf.* Diog. Laert., III, 52: 'Where he has a firm grasp, Plato expounds his own view and refutes the false one, but if the subject is obscure, he suspends judgement. His own views are expounded by four persons, Socrates, Timaeus,

the Athenian Stranger (in the *Laws*), the Eleatic Stranger (in the *Statesman* and *Sophist*).'

37 Diog. Laert., III, 37.

38 Cicero, *Brutus*, XXXI, 121.

39 Diog. Laert., V, 9 (Life of Aristotle). He was seventeen when he came to Plato.

40 Cicero, *Tusculanos*, I, xvii, 39.

41 See Cicero, *De Natura Deorum*, II, xii, 32.

42 Quintilian, *Institutio Oratoria*, X, i, 81.

43 Diog. Laert., III, 25: 'The eyes of all the Greeks were turned towards him.' The tradition concerning Plato's life has it that Plato, before joining Socrates, had been an athlete (a champion wrestler) and had participated in all four of the major Panhellenic games, including the Olympic. This story, however, relates to his return from the third Sicilian voyage, when he met Dion at Olympia. Compare Aelian, *Varia Historia*, IV, 9, where Plato visits the Olympic games incognito and associates freely with people assembled there, who are delighted by the company of this 'stranger'. A fuller source for this anecdote has not been found.

44 This story is told of Antimachus of Colophon, author of a long epic poem on the Theban cycle. See Cicero, *Brutus*, LI, 191.

45 Diog. Laert., III, 18; see Plato, *Epistles*, III and *passim*. Cf. *Epistles*, VII, 334D: 'Despotic power benefits neither rulers nor subjects, but is an altogether deadly experience for themselves, their children and their children's children.'

46 Diog. Laert., II, 78 (Life of Aristippus).

47 *Ibid.*, III, 24.

48 *Ibid.*, II, 41, (Life of Socrates); Olympiodorus, *Life of Plato*, I, 3. See *Prolegomena to Platonic Philosophy*, I, 3 (*op. cit.*, p. 8).

49 The sole source for this anecdote is Valerius Maximus, *Factorum et Dictorum Memorabilium*, IV, i, 2.

50 Diog. Laert., IV, 6–15.

51 Plutarch, *Life of Dion, passim*.

52 Philiscus of Miletus (*c.* 400–325 BC), a rhetorician who studied under Isocrates. Only fragments of his writings survive including the *Life of Lycurgus* (*Frag. Graec. Hist.*, III, 496 F9).

53 For this anecdote see Pseudo-Lucian, *In Praise of Demosthenes*, 47.

54 Demosthenes, *Letters*, V (to Heracleodorus), now regarded as spurious.

55 Diog. Laert., IV, 2 (Life of Speusippus). The Dionysius referred to is Dionysius the Younger of Syracuse.

56 *Ibid.*, IV, 1–2 (Life of Speusippus).

57 *Ibid.*, IV, 11 (Life of Xenocrates).

58 Many of the following anecdotes are outside the mainstream tradition of Plato's life, and come possible from a *florilegium* or *gnomologium* accessible to Ficino.

59 Diog. Laert., IV, 6: Xenocrates was slow and clumsy.

60 *Ibid.*, III, 35. The friend was Antisthenes.

61 *Ibid.*, VI, 53 (Life of Diogenes).

62 Plato gives advice to students in Stobaeus, 2, 31, 62; and in MSS Gnom. Vat. 433, 449; Cod. Vat. Graec. 742, f. 67^v and 633, f. 121^v.

63 Diog. Laert., III, 38.

64 *Ibid.*, III, 39.

65 Plato, *Timaeus*, 69D, *voluptas esca malorum;* quoted in Cicero, *De Senectute*, XIII, 44.

66 Diog. Laert., III, 40; Plato, *Laws*, II, 663E. For Demodocus see Plato, *Theages.*

67 See Plato, *Statesman*, 275B *et passim*, where a distinction is made between the function of a true statesman and that of other callings such as merchants, husbandmen *etc*: 'He alone of shepherds . . . has the care of human beings.'

68 *Cf.* Plato, *Statesman*, 275C: 'The statesmen who are now on earth seem to be much more like their subjects in character, and much more nearly to partake of their breeding and education.'

69 *Cf.* Plato, *Phaedo*, 66B–67, for the condition of the soul in the body, and Plato, *Theaetetus*, 176B for the instruction to fly from evil in order to become like God.

70 See note 10 above.

71 Diog. Laert., II, 81 (Life of Aristippus).

72 Jerome, *Letters* LIII, 1 (to Paulinus).

73 Plato, *Timaeus*, 27C: 'All men . . . who have any degree of right feeling, at the beginning of every enterprise, whether small or great, always call upon God.'

74 Lactantius, *Divine Institutes*, III, xix (*Pat. Lat.*, 6). The same story is told of Socrates and Thales. See Diog. Laert., I, 33 (Life of Thales).

75 See Plato's assertion that there are no writings of his own; all are those of an idealised Socrates: Plato, *Epistles*, II, 314C.

76 Diog. Laert., III, 8 (Life of Plato). *Cf.* the threefold division of philosophy into physics, ethics and dialectic described by Diogenes in the prologue to his *Lives* (Diog. Laert., I, 18). Plato is credited with dividing philosophy into three parts—natural, moral and rational. Previous to this the division was two-fold, the active represented by Socrates and the contemplative represented by Pythagoras. See Augustine, *City of God*, VIII, iv.

77 *Cf.* Plato, *Meno*, 81CD, the 'sacred words'; Plato, *Laws*, X, 903B–905C; *Epistles*, VII, 335.

78 Augustine, *Contra Academicos*, III, xx, 43.

79 Dionysius the Areopagite (Pseudo-Dionysius) in the *Divine Names* introduces a Plotinian concept of the godhead into his exposition of the Trinity.

80 *Cf.* Eusebius, *Praeparatio Evangelica*, XI–XIII; Cyrillus Alexandrinus, *Contra Julianum*, I, 29 *et passim*. (Eusebius of Caesarea, historian and theologian *c*. AD 260–340; Cyril of Alexandria, patriarch and theologian, *d*. AD 444).

81 Augustine, *De Vera Religione*, IV, vii (*Pat. Lat.*, 34).

82 Augustine, *Confessions* VII, ix: the Word or Λόγος, *John* I:1–5.

83 Augustine, *City of God*, II, xiv. (Cornelius Labeo, pagan writer, AD 300, works not extant).

84 Marcus Varro: Roman historian (116–27 BC), whose lost encyclopaedia of learning, the *Antiquities*, is quoted by Augustine in the *City of God, passim*.

85 Apuleius, *De Platone.* I, 2.

86 For this, see Aeneas Gazaeus, *Theophrastus* (dialogue on the immortality of the soul). This work was translated into Latin by Ambrogio Traversari in 1456. Gazaeus was a Platonist and later a Christian of the 5th century AD.

87 Seneca, *Epistles*, LVIII, 31; Olympiodorus, *Life of Plato*. See *Prolegomena to Platonic Philosophy*, I, 6.

88 Cicero, *De Senectute*, V, 13.

89 Seneca, *Epistles*, LVIII, 31.

90 Diog. Laert., III, 2.

91 Ammonius Hermiae (attrib.), *Vita Aristotelis*, II, 5, quoted in G4. D. L. Stockton suggests this translation:
'This altar Aristotle did to Plato raise,
a man whom Heav'n forbids the base should praise.'

92 Olympiodorus, *Commentarium in Georgia Platonis*, XLI, 9.

93 For these epitaphs see Diog. Laert., III, 43-5.

94 A similar description of Ficino as a healer of men's souls is said to have been given by Cosimo: see Ficino, *Opera*, p. 493 (dedicatory letter to *De Vita Libri Tres*) and Corsi, *Life of Marsilio Ficino*, V; see page 138.

95 Diog. Laert., III, 25.

96 The reference is undoubtedly meant to include the contemporary burlesque poet Luigi Pulci who had lampooned Ficino and Plato in his poem *Morgante*.

97 Diog. Laert., III, 29 *seq.*

98 See Diog. Laert., II, 49 (Life of Xenophon).

99 *Ibid.*, III, 29.

100 See Ammonius Hermiae, *Vita Aristotelis*, I, 43, relating Aristotle's description of himself as 'the friend of Socrates but more the friend of truth.'

101 See note 91 above.

102 Olympiodorus, *Commentarium in Georgia Platonis*, XLI, 9.

103 Apuleius, *Apologia*, 64.
The first and shorter version of the *Vita Platonis* (V10) ends with these words: 'Let that be sufficient on the life of Plato. To you, most noble gentlemen, who have thought fit to honour this speech of mine with your presence, I render great thanks. Immortal God, would that I might bring back the immortals.' (*De vita platonis iam satis dictum sit. Vobis autem viri praestantissimi, qui meam hanc orationem vestra praesentia honestare dignati estis, ingentes gratias habeo. Immortalis deus immortales referam*).

20

1 Ficino's book *Disputatio Contra Iudicium Astrologorum* (Against the Judgement of Astrologers) (*Sup. Fic.*, II, pp. 11-76).

2 The reference is possibly to Tommaso Benci, brother of Ginevra Benci (see note on Bembo). In 1463 Tommaso made an Italian translation of Ficino's Latin version of Hermes Trismegistus' *Pimander*.

22

1 Virgil, *Aeneid*, VI, 687–8.
2 See letter 13 in praise of philosophy, above.

23

1 Ficino also personifies Echo as a celestial quality in the third book of *De Vita Libri Tres*, xxi, (*Opera* I, pp. 563–4).
2 See letter 13, above.

24

1 Ovid, *Heroides*, I, 12.
2 I Corinthians 13: 7–8.
3 I John 4: 18.
4 Augustine, *Confessions*, IV, ix.

25

1 This letter was written about 24th June, 1477, as appears from MS S, which adds the following: *Tu Antoni vale. Florentia II nonas octobris*, with an accompanying letter to Antonio Ivani of Sarzana. See *Sup. Fic.*, II, p. 91; *ibid.*, I, p. 31.

26

1 Virgil, *Eclogues*, III, 108.
2 See pp. 56–57 for the effect of a sudden transition from the cave to sunlight and vice versa. An irony is intended.
3 Plato, *Republic*, VII, 514A–518B. Ficino quotes this passage on the allegory of the cave, using a differently worded translation, in the *Platonic Theology*, VI, ii, ed. Marcel, Vol. I, pp. 232–4.
4 Homer, *Odyssey*, XI, 489.

27

1 This letter was translated into Italian by Ficino and included in his *Sermoni Morali della Stultitia et Miseria degli Uomini* addressed to Jacopo Guicciardini. See note 1, to letter 1, above.
2 Ficino's universe, which is based partly on the neoplatonic system, is divided into four hierarchies: (1) the Cosmic Mind or Nous, the Supercelestial Realm which is incorruptible; (2) the Cosmic Soul or *Anima Mundi*, the Celestial World of Pure Causes; (3) the Realm of Nature, compounded of form and matter,

which is connected to the Celestial World by the *Spiritus Mundanus* or *Humanus*;
(4) the Realm of Matter which is formless and gross. The 'middle region' in
this letter would seem to refer to the Realm of Nature and *Spiritus Mundanus*.
See Panofsky, *Studies in Iconology*, Oxford 1939, ch. 5: 'The Neoplatonic Movement in Florence and Northern Italy'.

3 Plato, *Republic*, IX 588c–589c.
4 Plato, *Timaeus*, 69c–72c.
5 Plato, *Phaedrus*, 246, 253DE.
6 The giant Antaeus, symbolising desire, was invincible so long as he remained
  in contact with his mother earth. He forced strangers to wrestle with him and
  then slew them. Hercules, lifting him from the earth, crushed him to death in
  the air. Fulgentius, *Mythologiae*, II, 4.
7 Plato, *Phaedo*, 84A.
8 *Cf.* Plato, *Phaedo*, 81B–82A and Ficino, *Platonic Theology*, XVII, iv, ed. Marcel,
  Vol. III, pp. 167–74, where transmigration and the soul's appetites are discussed.
9 Plato, *Phaedrus*, 230A.

29

1 *Disputatio Contra Iudicium Astrologorum*. See *Sup. Fic.*, II, pp. 11–76.

30

1 For Capella and Francesco d'Este see Notes on Ficino's Correspondents. Panfilo
  corresponded with Poliziano. See P. O. Kristeller, *Iter Italicum*, I, Index.

31

1 See letter 32.
2 A pun: *barbarus* in Latin means barbarian.

32

1 For an Italian translation of this letter see article by Alessandra Canavero Tar-
  abochia, 'L'amicizia nell'epistolario di Marsilio Ficino' in *Rivista di Filosofia
  Neo-Scolastica*, Vol. 67, 1975.
2 I Corinthians 13:5.
3 Psalms 133:1.

33

1 This letter was written in September 1477, as appears from MS S, which adds:
  Vale. Florentia VIII Kal. Octobris.

34

1 For this idea see Plato, *Laws*, IV, 721C: 'Now mankind is coeval with all time, and is ever following, and will ever follow the course of time; and so men are immortal, because they leave children's children behind them, and partake of immortality in the unity of generation'.

2 Compare Plato, *Phaedo*, 97C–98C, where Socrates describes his disappointment on finding that Anaxagoras was not capable of teaching him the causes of existence. Socrates had two wives: Xanthippe and Myrto; Diog. Laert., II, 26 (Life of Socrates).

3 See Augustine, *De Vera Religione*, iii, 5.

4 Plato, *Laws*, IV, 721C; VI, 774A.

5 Hermes Trismegistus, *Pimander*, II, 17a.

6 *Cf.* Aristotle, *Politics*, I, 1253A.

7 Virgil, *Aeneid*, I, 630.

35

1 Juno, Queen of the Gods and Mistress of Heaven. As the female counterpart of Jupiter she presided over all human affairs, and often made use of Minerva as her messenger. She was patroness of power and riches.

2 Virgil, *Aeneid*, VI, 128 . . . *superasque evadere ad auras.*

3 Minerva, as the Goddess of Wisdom and the Liberal Arts, was said to have been born from the head or mind of Jove himself, *i.e.* the source of wisdom. Fulgentius, *Mythologiae*, II, 1.

4 Plato, *Apology*, 21B.

5 Plato, *Phaedrus*, 279D.

6 For this anecdote see Hippocrates, *Letters*, 17, (to Damagetes) in *Works*, ed. Littré, Vol. IX, p. 349 *seq.*

7 See Diog. Laert., II, 40 (Life of Socrates).

8 The familiar image of the weeping and laughing philosophers, Heraclitus and Democritus, frequently mentioned by Ficino: see *Letters*, Vol. I, letter 58. A painting depicting this subject adorned the walls of Ficino's academy.

36

1 This letter was written shortly before the Pazzi Conspiracy, in which Bracciolini played a leading part.

2 Ficino is referring to John of Salisbury's *Policraticus*, V, i, which contains the text of this letter of Plutarch to Trajan. The letter is now considered to be part of a lost pseudo-classical work entitled *Institutio Traiani* which cannot be ascribed to Plutarch himself. This letter was very popular both in the Middle Ages and the Renaissance period and is quoted in numerous manuscripts not connected with the *Policraticus*. See Kristeller, *Studies*, p. 40 and note 36; see also article by

H. Liebeschütz, 'John of Salisbury and Pseudo Plutarch' in *Journal of the Warburg and Courtauld Institutes* (6), 1943.

3 Seneca, who was Nero's tutor before he became Emperor, was accused of having provided no antidote to Nero's vicious propensities, and even of having encouraged them. See Tacitus, *Annales*, XIII–XIV; Dion Cassius, *Historia*, LXI, 10.

4 The Emperor Domitian committed his sister's grandsons to the care of Quintilian. Nothing further is known about this episode. See Quintilian, *Institutio Oratoria*, IV, proem.

5 Alcibiades, the Athenian general and disciple of Socrates, who resumed his evil ways on leaving Socrates. Socrates was blamed.

37

1 See letter 29, note 1.

2 The substance of the argument from the beginning of this paragraph up to here is taken from Aulus Gellius, *Attic Nights,* XIV, 1, 36.

3 Seneca, *Oedipus*, 980. The original reads '*fatis agimur, cedite fatis*' (We are moved by the Fates; yield to them).

4 Lucretius, *De Rerum Natura*, I, 79. Ficino has substituted *impietas* (wickedness) where the original reads *religio*.

38

1 Ficino's 'Life of Plato'; see letter 19, above.

2 Athens fell to the Turks in 1458.

3 See Notes on Ficino's Correspondents, under Bandini and Corvinus.

4 This birthday festival was held on 7th November, 1468: see *Letters*, Vol. I, letter 107; see also note 3 to letter 19, above.

5 This letter, which was written between September 1477 and January 1478, was originally included in the fifth book of *Letters*, as appears from MSS G1, R10 and M9. See *Sup. Fic.*, I,c.

39 ·

1 This work is the *Secunda Platonicae Sapientiae Clavis* in *Opera*, p. 688. See also Marcel, *Théologie Platonicienne*, Vol. III, appendix, pp. 297–300).

2 *De Amore, Oratio Septima*, IV (ed. Marcel, p. 246). 'And as the sun, which is the heart of the universe, sends out from its orbit its light, and through its light its own strength to lower things, so the heart of our body . . . pours out . . . sparks of light through the various single parts, but especially through the eyes' (tr. S. R. Jayne, *Marsilio Ficino's Commentary on Plato's Symposium*).

Ficino is suggesting that his knowledge is passing through Bandini and Bathory who are, in this context, his eyes. By the same image he implies that he is receiving information from Hungary through his two followers.

For a similar idea see *Timaeus*, 45.

3 Originally Ficino included this letter in the sixth book of *Letters*, as appears from MSS R10 and M9. See *Sup. Fic.*, I,c.

Ficino, on the 1st October, 1480, dedicated Books III and IV of the *Epistolae* to King Matthias Corvinus of Hungary (see *Letters*, Vol. 2, letter 1) and for this occasion added these last two letters—both addressed to friends in Hungary— to Book IV as well as letter 37 addressed to Petrus Pannonius, Archbishop of Koloswar.

The following text is added at the end of G4: *Transcripsi hoc opus ego Sebastianus Salvinus Amitinus Marsilii Ficini philosophi suo seculo singularis, non quia scriptor ipse sim, cum iam pridem fuerim professor artium, in sacra pagina magister licet indignus, sed ut morem gererem Francisco iunio magnanimo civi tamque insigni philosopho patrono musarum Marsilio Ficino nanciscererque occasionem commendandi me ipsum iterum atque iterum invicto regi Pannoniae, ut me habeat servum undique paratissimum.*

'I, Sebastiano Salvini, cousin of that outstanding philosopher of his age, Marsilio Ficino, have transcribed this work. Not because I am a scribe, for I have long been a master of arts and theology, albeit an unworthy one, but so that I might carry out the will of Francesco Giugni, a most worthy citizen, and of so great a philosopher and patron of the muses, Marsilio Ficino; and also so that I might take the opportunity of boldly commending myself to the invincible King of Hungary so that he should have me as his servant, well-prepared in every respect.'

The following text is added to R10 at the end of the fourth book of letters: *Transcripsit manu propria preclarum hoc opus Sebastianus Salvinus amitinus eiusdem Marsilii Ficini philosophi insignis, theologie professor et artium amicitia ad transcribendum ductus.*

'Sebastiano Salvini, professor of theology and the arts, cousin of the same renowned Marsilio Ficino, with his own hand, copied out this remarkable work, being led by friendship to transcribe it.'

Notes on the Latin Text

It is not intended that these notes should be exhaustive or should supplant a study proper to a critical edition. They have been prepared:

(a) to give the key variants;

(b) to allow anyone using the Basle edition (the most accessible) to correct the corruptions of that text;

(c) to indicate the path this translation has attempted to follow.

A few points need to be made. As stated in the Preface:

(i) we give in these notes the comparison between the most important manuscripts and the three most important printed editions. The most important manuscripts are three in number (G4, R10, Be) for the book as a whole, with an additional two (M7, V10) of prime importance for letters 18 and 19. The sigla of the manuscripts and of these printed editions are identified in the Preface (see p. xiii).

(ii) we have followed G4 as generally the most reliable source, except in letters 18 and 19 where we consider M7 to be the most important manuscript. Occasions where we have departed from this are mentioned.

In the collation for each note it will be seen that the sigla are given in tabular form and in a definite order which reflects our opinion of the relative importance of the manuscripts. The spelling, punctuation and capitals given are those of the main manuscript or edition quoted. If B or some other source has an error or a corruption which is meaningless, it is left out of the collation.

The orthography we have used for the Latin in these notes is as near as we have been able to attain to that used by Ficino (for instance: *Marsilij, uiuit, Vt*). The long 'i' ('j') was introduced by the Renaissance humanists themselves (and was used by Ficino) to indicate a semi-consonantal quality. In other parts of this book the orthography is that now standard in modern Latin (*e.g. Marsilii, vivit, Ut*). This course has been adopted so as not to mislead those who may be unused to the orthography of the Renaissance humanists.

To clarify the form of address in the letters, we point as an example to the address of letter 31. In G4 this reads *Marsilius ficinus florentinus Hermolao Barbaro ueneto. S.d.* We include *florentinus* and *S.d.* in the translation only when G4 has them. The same applies to *Vale* if it appears at the end of a letter.

For letter 19 the major discrepancies between V10 (which was an early and considerably shorter version) and the other manuscripts will not be mentioned in this collation—only those parts of V10 which in general correspond with the other texts will be commented upon here. The full collation will await the critical edition.

1

a	(on page facing Letter 1)	
	G4 R10	have the words *Incipit quartus liber epistolarum Marsilij Ficini florentini* above the heading of the first letter.
	Be V	read likewise but without *Incipit*
	B P	as Be but in reverse order, thus: *Marsilij Ficini florentini, Epistolarum Liber IV* Be is followed here as G4 contains Books III & IV and thus required *Incipit* whereas in our edition these two books have been published separately.
b	G4 R10 Be V P	read *possit quot omnes*
c	V B P	read *Marsilius Ficinus Florentinus Laurentio* but G4R10Be omit *florentinus*. However, since this is the first letter and the beginning of the book, the style seems to require the words 'of Florence' at this point.
d	G4 R10 Be V	read *pythagoras, ne cerebrum*
e	G4 R10	read *curis cor urerent* but Be VBP omit *cor*
f	G4 R10	read *cuncta proueniunt, in* but Be VBP have *perueniunt*
g	G4 R10 Be	read *aliud nobis est* but VBP omit *nobis*
h	G4 R10 Be V	read *Forma quoque roburque*
i	G4 R10 Be V	read *agriculturam nostram, sed*
j	G4 R10 V B P	read *debeamus. Sementem* but Be reads *debeamus. Sed mentem*

2

a	R10	reads *ficinus comphilosopho suo* but leaves a gap between *ficinus* and *comphilosopho*; Be leaves a clear gap after *suo*, both presumably for the name.
b	G4 R10 Be V	read *quae ingrati nos*
c	R10 Be V B P	read *rationi obsequare pareasque consilio. Postquam uero diligenti rationi* but G4 omits the words from *obsequare* to *rationi* (inclusive), clearly an error in transcription.

4

a	G4 R10 Be	read *medicina morborum est* but VBP have *malorum*
b	G4 R10 Be V P	read *ad ima descendunt*
c	G4 R10 Be V P	read *patriam amando prorsus et adorando.*

5

a	G4 R10 Be	read *ficinus et Joannes Caualcantes Georgio* whereas VBP omit *et Joannes Caualcantes*
b	G4 R10 V	read *arbitror. Qui* but Be has colon and BP comma. These latter readings are preferred.

7

a	G4 R10 Be P	read *Qualis in se quisque est,*
b	G4 R10 Be V P	read *diuina inuitos assequitur.*
c	G4 R10 Be	read *colores lineasque pictores*

8

a	G4 R10 Be V P	read *meum alit pacem*
b	G4 R10 Be V P	read *suaue redolens, insipido*
c	G4 R10 Be V	read *dei. Haec nobis*
d	VBP	add *Florentiae* after the date.

9

a	Be	reads at end of heading *muta: Apologus quidam de difficultate humanae uitae.*
b	G4 R10 Be V P	read *continue ducant, uenit in mentem ludus quidam eiusmodi,*
c	G4 R10 Be V	read *quaecunque attigerint, portanda*
d	G4 R10 Be	read *Tales o amici*
e	G4 R10 Be	read *animae id est rationem,*

10

a	G4 R10 Be	read *raptu in tertium caelum*
b	G4 R10 Be	read *supercelesti lumine ad*
c	Be V P	read *tam qui obnixe quaeritat, quam qui* but G4 omits the first *qui.* The former reading is preferred.

d	G4 R10 Be V P	read *meam hanc suamque*
e	G4 R10 Be V	read *suorum radijs illustrauerit.*
f	G4 R10	read *Neque coram ut* but Be BP have *charam*, (V *caram*) which is preferred.
g	G4 R10 Be	read *beatissimum pinxi caelestis* but VBP have *depinxi*
h	G4 R10 Be	read *instar numenij passim eleusina sacra uulgaui.*
i	G4	reads *syrus adyta caelestium* and R10Be have *adita* but VBP have *abdita* which is preferred.
j	R10	reads *Sed edipus arcana* and BP have *Oedipi* but G4Be V have *edipis*

11

a	G4 R10 Be V	read *ut deo placeas* but BP has *placeat* which is preferred.
b	G4 R10 Be V P	read *Vt familiarem epistolam*
c	G4 R10 Be V P	read *consilium quam ratio*
d	G4 R10 Be V	read *sentitur. Intimum tamen*
e	G4 R10 Be V P	read *mihi placeat bonum*

12

a	R10 Be V B P	read *nihil uel mirabilius uel* but G4 omits first *uel*
b	G4 R10 Be V P	read *Quando singularis doctrina*
c	G4 R10	read *declamatiunculas offeret: quarum* but Be BP have *offert* which is preferred.

13

a	G4 R10 Be	read *saepe ijs qui in* but VBP have second word *his* and omit *qui*
b	G4 R10 Be V P	read *posse diffidam. Neque*
c	V B P	read *eius aut egregias* but G4R10Be omit *aut*
d	G4 R10 Be	read *,cuius splendore explicamus omnia,* but BP put comma before *omnia* and V has no punctuation mark.
e	G4 R10 Be	read *accedunt propinquius,* but VBP put punctuation mark before *propinquius*
f	G4 R10 Be	read *huic nostrae trinitati* but V has *nrae* with an abbreviation mark above, which could signify as G4 or possibly *naturae* which BP

g G4 R10 Be   read *progressionibusque disserit, deo* but VBP have *dixerit*

h G4   reads *dirigimus, deoque beatitudinis* but R10Be VBP have *deo quoque* which is preferred.

i G4 R10 Be   read *donis rectissime utitur*. VBP have *certissime*

14

a G4   Be   read *quae sunt discenda* and R10 reads *discenda sunt*

b G4 R10 Be V   read *quo profecta sunt*

c G4 R10 Be V   read *percipit ueritate, ueritatis*

d G4 R10   have a punctuation mark between each of these names, except between *Dioclem* and *carystium*

e G4 R10   read *Hoseanem* and Be reads *Hoscanem* but VBP read *Hostanem* which is followed.

f G4 R10 Be   read *duae ac uiginti*

g G4 R10 Be V   read *impendit? Sabor quoque*

h G4   reads *cuius ut principia* but R10Be VBP read *cuius ue principia* which is preferred.

i   B P   read *Phoebus, ut in epistolis* and Be V likewise but with bracket before *ut*. G4 has no bracket and omits *ut* whereas R10 has no bracket but has *ut* added. Readings of the other MSS cited and of edd. preferred to G4.

j G4   reads *id est physicis rationibus* but Be BP have third word *philosophicis* which is preferred. R10 V have abbreviations which are uncertain.

k After the end of letter 14 G4R10 set out the following (G4 in red letter):

Secuntur deinceps declamationes quatuor.
Prima incipit,   *Siquis agricola non etc.*
Secunda.   *Quaerenti mihi praecipuam hodie etc.*
Tertia.   *Quid tandiu uituperas homo etc.*
Quarta.   *Mandauit discipulis suis etc.*
Hae quatuor declamationes sunt in superioribus.
V follows G4 but adds *solum sine* after *non* in first 'incipit'.

15

a G4 R10 Be V	read *astronomo et poetae.* BP omit *et*

16

a G4 R10 Be V P	read *inuidae naturae damna*
b G4 R10 Be	read *ualitudinem ferunt ferme* but BP have *terunt*
c G4 R10 Be V P	read *ergo quidam possessionis*
d G4 R10 Be V	read *debeo deo. Quando* but BP omit *deo*
e G4	reads *est, infimi undique* but R10Be VBP have *infirmi* which is preferred.

17

a R10 Be V B P	read *mi Bernarde nihil* but G4 has *Bembe*
b G4 R10 Be V P	read *rapueris litteratos. Tu*
c V P	have date *xxv Aprilis. MCCCCLXXVII.* but G4R10Be have *XXVI Aprilis 1477* (B same but all in Roman numerals)

18

a M7 V10 G4 R10 Be V P	read *corruptioni obnoxia sunt*
b V10 G4 Be	read *partes, quae affectibus efferri solent, domitas* whilst all the MSS and edd. presently cited have this text, the punctuation (which here seems important) is not identical. M7, however, does have second comma as above.
c B P	read *temperantiae, libertatis sit* but M7V10G4R10Be V have *liberalitatis*
d M7	reads *animus: Gymnasticae ludis* and G4 reads likewise, except with a stop (to be taken as a comma) and lower case 'g'.
e M7 V10 G4 R10 Be V P	read *.Interim optimarum legum*
f G4	reads *moderatus paratusque reddatur.* but M7V10R10Be VBP have *pacatusque* which is preferred.
g M7 V10 G4 R10 Be V	read *numeris, planis figuris et solidis*
h M7 V10 G4 R10 Be V P	read *quam solidae. Solida*
i B P	read *motus suscipit. Postrema* but M7V10G4R10Be V have *suspicit*

j   V10 G4 R10 Be V   read *intelligantur: ex* and M7 has a full stop. The punctuation here seems to mark a clear break.

k   V B P   read *bonum, unde* but V10G4R10Be read *bonum, inde* and M7 agrees with the latter but punctuation is a full stop.

l   G4   reads *leges intuitum habuerunt.* but M7V10R10Be VBP have *initium* which is preferred.

m M7 V10 G4 R10 Be   read *ex ipsa dei similitudine* but VBP omit *ipsa*

n   G4 R10   read *sapientiaque concurrerent. Apud* and V10 has this but with second *re* under–dotted which may have been missed in a transcription. M7 VBP have *concurrent* which is preferred.

o   V10 G4 R10 Be   read *superna, tenebrisque ad* and M7 likewise except *tenebris* but VBP read *superna, a tenebrisque ad*

p M7 V10 G4 R10 Be   read *uero facultates et disciplinae quas narrauimus*

q M7 V10   end with *hominum gubernatio.*

r   G4 R10 Be V   P   read *Juliano Burgo nostro*

19

a   G4 R10 Be V   read *intueamur : ut et*

b M7   V B P   have heading *Genealogia et Genesis Platonis* and Be likewise but with spelling error in *Genealogia*. R10 has the heading in the margin. G4 omits the heading. M7 followed. The 'De Vita Platonis' part of M7 begins here.

c M7   G4 R10 Be V   P   read *a Nereo et*

d   B P   read *fuit, at Glauconem* but M7G4R10Be V have *atque*

e   G4 R10 Be   read *uero Aristoni nupta* but VBP have *Aristone* which is followed.

f   B P   read *Ariston Platonis a Codro* but G4R10 V add *pater* after *Platonis* also M7 looks as if it reads as G4 but uses a shorthand form. Be reads as G4 etc. but without preposition.

g   G4 R10 Be V   read *Julius firmius astronomus* but BP have *firmicus* which is followed.

h M7   G4 R10 Be V   P   read *Hanc genesim Julius*

i M7 V10 G4 R10   read *per somnum oloris pullum sibi* but VBP have *somnium* as first noun, which is followed, and B has *pullulum* as third noun.

j		G4		reads *pennis, expansis alis,* (punctuation)
k	M7 V10 G4 R10 Be V	P		read *et hermogeni parmenidis*
l	M7			reads *ante nuncupatus fuisset* but R10Be VBP have *nominatus* and G4 has *uocatus*
m	M7	G4 R10		read *sub ceruice gibbosum, eum aliquantulum deformabat.* Be reads likewise but adds *nescio quid* after *ceruice.* V reads as M7, except penultimate word *aliquantum.* BP have *uertice* as first noun, otherwise as G4.
n		G4 R10		read *forte Amiceris cirenaicus* but M7V10Be VBP have *Anniceris*
o			VBP	read *cognouisset et quae* but M7V10G4R10Be omit *et*
p	M7	Be V	P	have heading *Secunda nauigatio* which G4 omits. R10 puts heading in the margin.
q		G4		has no heading but begins *Tertio* with rubric reverse indentation. Likewise other MSS and edd. cited have no heading, except Be which has *Tertia Nauigatio.* Be is followed.
r	M7	G4 R10		read *ab utroque iterum atque iterum obsecratus.* VBP omit *atque iterum*
s	V10			has the following addition in margin *et ipse quadrigis abhis egredientem excepit.* It seems certain that *abhis* should read *albis* which is the reading of all other MSS cited and VBP.
t		G4 R10 Be V		read *detractauit. Cum uero Plato* and M7 P read likewise except first word *detrectauit*
u	M7	G4		read *Tarentinus Salmiscum misit ad Dionysium oratorem* and R10 reads likewise but with a comma after *Dionysium.* VP read as M7G4 but have *Salmuscum*
v	M7	G4 R10 Be V B P		read *exceptus est in patria.* G4 omits *in*
w	V10			reads *Maledimum* and M7 reads *Mededimum* but an 'l' appears to have been written over the first 'd'. G4Be have *Meledimum* and R10 VBP *Mededimum*
x	M7 V10 G4 R10 Be			read *Augustinus perhibet castus.* V has an unclear abbreviation of *per* whence BP obtained *prohibet*
y	M7	G4 R10 Be V		read *uulgus a crimine* but BP omit the preposition.
z	M7	G4 R10 Be V	P	read *ad parentes reuersus*
aa	M7			reads *inquit, Cede tu* with a mark under first vowel of middle word, a diphthong sign, indicating *Caede.* G4R10Be VB spell the verb *Cede.* P alone, besides M7, has *Caede* which is followed.

bb		B		reads *sunt exponunt, & nos satis* and P likewise but with a comma after *sunt*. Be reads *sunt exponant: satis* whilst G4 reads *sunt exponantur, satis* and V likewise except colon in place of comma. R10 reads as G4, except that there appears to be a comma before *exponantur* as well as afterwards.
cc	M7			reads *jocundiores gratiosioresque redderentur* but G4R10Be VBP have *gratioresque*
dd				in this list of names the following require comment:
		VB		read *Anicles: Heraclites,* (B has a comma between the words). P has *Heraclitus* as second word. M7G4R10Be read *Anicles Heracleotes,* and V10 as M7 but second word reads *Heracliteotes*
		V		reads *hebeon: Lampsacenus: Pithori:* BP the same, except with commas. M7V10G4 Be read *Hebeon Lampsacenus. Piton.* In M7 the 'n' of *Piton* is written with a break, so that it could be misread as *Pithori*
		VBP		read *Demetrius. Amphipolites. Heraclides. Ponticus* and M7V10R10Be read likewise but have only one punctuation mark, that between *Amphipolites* and *Heraclides*
		VBP		read *axithea phyasia* but M7V10R10Be read *axiothea Phlyasia*
ee	M7 V10 G4	Be V	P	read *bono. Conuiuium de amore.*
ff	M7 V10 G4 R10 Be V		P	read *Lysidem de amicitia.*
gg	M7	G4 R10 Be		read *epinomi Plato ipse suo disserit ore* but V10 V have verb *dixerit* and BP *dixit*. V. has mark over the last i of *epinomi* indicating case ending omitted, BP supplying ending with *Epinomide*
hh	V10	R10 Be VBP		read *libris Socratis* but G4 has *Socraticis* as the second word. M7 is unclear. V10 is followed.
ii	M7 V10 G4 R10 Be V			read *illustres ad externas*
jj	M7	G4 R10 Be V	P	read *Cicerone scribitur. Malo*
kk	M7	G4 R10 Be		read *Divina quadam sapientia* but VBP omit *quadam*
ll	M7			reads *omitti cerneres:et* and G4R10 likewise but with the past participle spelt *obmicti* and Be V likewise but spelt *obmitti*
mm	M7	G4 R10 Be		read *gratia ad Olympia* but VBP omit *ad* which is followed.

nn	M7	G4 R10 Be V	P	read *diversorio conquiescebant. Cum*
oo	M7	G4 R10 Be V		read *nec quispiam praeter* but BP have indefinite pronoun *quisquam*
pp	M7	G4 R10 Be		read *fuerit, declarant eius* but VBP have *indicant*
qq		G4		reads *illi assentiretur.* but M7 has *assentaretur* for the verb, which R10Be VBP follow and this is preferred.
rr		G4 R10		read *Crobylus accusator improbus* and M7 reads likewise but spells the name *Crobilus* whereas V has M7 spelling of the name but follows this with *accusato.* BP as V. G4R10 are followed here.
ss	M7	R10		read *in tolerandis periculis* with which G4 Be agree but spell middle word *tollerandis.* VBP join the first two words together.
tt	M7	G4 R10 Be V		read *sim uiri Athenienses* but BP omit *uiri*
uu	M7	G4 R10 Be		read *Verum tyrannici iudices* but VBP have *tyranni*
vv	M7	R10 Be		read *illi malae mentis* and G4 has *male* which must be taken as *malae*
ww	M7	R10 Be V B P		read *in Platonem Xenocratis* but G4 has *Platone* apparently from a misreading by Salvini of M7 which gives an unclear abbreviation.
xx		G4 R10 Be		read *hoc abscidet.* It looks as if M7 has *abscidet* and that any apparent abbreviation mark is, in fact, part of a line of writing, probably in another hand, at right angles to and underneath M7 text. BP have *abscindet.*
yy	M7	G4 R10 Be V		read *Hui qualem equum, qualemque asinum* In BP the sentence before *Hui* appears as a second heading but should form part of the main body of the text. Likewise V has this as a form of heading.
zz		G4 R10 Be V		read *nequaquam. Cui mirum* but BP have *Quid* as middle word, which is preferred.
ab	M7	Be		read *sola illae cernuntur* and G4R10 V have *ille* which must be read as *illae*
cb	M7	G4 R10 Be V	P	read *uita seuerus, nescio*
db	M7	G4 R10 Be		read *Ad iuuenes crebro*
eb	M7	G4 R10 Be V	P	read *saepissime incendebat, Contrariam*
fb		G4 R10 V		read *subita penitentia sequitur dolorque perpetuus. Illius autem breues* and M7Be read likewise except for spelling *poenitentia* and P reads as M7 but omits *autem*

gb			B P	read *intuerentur, ab eiusmodi* but M7G4R10Be V omit *ab*
hb	M7			reads *extimescerunt. Demodoco de* whereas G4R10 have *De modo eo, de* at beginning of sentence. B has *Demonco de* and P has *Demonico de*, both presumably interpretations of V which has *De mōco de*. Be reads *De modico de*. M7 is followed.
ib	M7		R10 Be V B P	read *carpenti, quod non* but G4 has *quam*—clearly an error.
jb	M7	G4 R10	V B P	read *uero uerisimilia. Dormire* but Be has *uerissima*
kb	M7	G4 R10 Be		read *Nam cum et* whereas VBP have *dum*
lb	M7		R10 Be V B P	read *fugientes persequitur, captus* but G4 has *prosequitur*
mb	M7			reads *composita scribit non* and G4 likewise but with comma after *scribit*. R10Be VBP read likewise but have punctuation mark before *scribit*
nb	M7		V B P	read *et qui eum confirmauerunt.* G4R10Be have *quidam* instead of *qui eum* (erroneously).
ob	M7	G4 R10 Be	P	read *ipsis preferendum esse*
pb	M7	G4		read *rerum adyta penetrauerit.* R10Be V have *adita* but BP *abdita* which is followed.
qb	M7	R10		read *lumine repperisse. Quod* and Be V read likewise but spell verb with one 'p'. G4, however, has *repetisse* which looks erroneous.
rb			Be P	read *ac lenis senectus* and M7 could well read *lenis*. G4R10 VB have *lenis*. Be is followed.
sb			V B P	read *uno et octuagesima aetatis anno* but Be omits *aetatis*. M7G4R10 read as Be but G4 has 80 in Arabic numerals and M7R10 have it in Roman numerals. The edd. are followed.
tb	M7	G4 R10	V B P	read *id platoni sobrietatis* but Be has *Platonis*
ub	M7	G4		the Greek quotation we have given reads the same as M7 and G4 but with οὐτ' instead of οὐδ' which was probably the intention of the original.
vb		G4		reads *dicauit: uiro quem nefas est* and M7Be P read likewise except with a punctuation mark after rather than before *uiro*. R10 reads as G4 but spells penultimate word *nephas*. BP read as R10 but without punctuation. G4 is followed.

wb M_7		read *sed praecipue epigrammata* but G_4R_{10} VBP have *praecipua* and Be has *praecipuae*
xb M_7	G_4 R_{10} Be V P	read *inuidiam superauerit. Secundi*
yb M_7	Be V B P	read *sunt plebei quidam* but G_4 has *phebaei* and R_{10} *phebei* but these last two look erroneous.
zb M_7	G_4 R_{10} Be V P	read *optimi cuiusque suorum*
ac M_7	G_4 R_{10} Be V	read *Platonem. Finxitque horum* but BP have *Finxit*
bc M_7	Be B P	read *sub praetextu laudis* although G_4 has *protestu* and R_{10} reads as G_4 but with the 's' in *protestu* amended to 'x'. V has *praetestu*
dc M_7	G_4 R_{10} Be V P	read *iudicio sapientum approbatissimam*

20

a G_4	Be	read *celestia ueri metiuntur* but R_{10} BP have *uere*

22

a	G_4 R_{10} Be V P	read *Bembo iurisconsulto et*
b	G_4 R_{10} Be V P	read *hodie a Marco*
c	G_4 R_{10} Be V	read *ab aequore Veneto*
d	G_4 R_{10} Be V	read *Sane eisdem maij* but BP have *eiusdem*
e	G_4 R_{10} Be	read *peruenisse. Mirabilem Bernarde* and V has the same but with an abbreviation mark over the 'e' to signify the adjective ending. This mark was presumably overlooked in preparing B, which P then copied.

23

a	G_4 R_{10} Be P	read *idem cogitat alter.*
b	G_4 R_{10} Be	read *hominem e celo dependens, tum in planam humanitatis faciem, tum in caeli concaua resilit, uicissim* and V reads likewise except for *humanitas* in place of genitive.
c	G_4 R_{10} Be	read *deo. Neque* but V has a colon in place of full stop. BP has a comma.
d	G_4 R_{10} Be	read *penitus atque tu et* but BP have *utrunque* in place of *atque tu*

24

a G4 R10   read *inceptaueram, atque* and Be reads likewise
                             but with a colon in place of the comma.
                             VBP have a full stop.

25

a G4 R10 Be V   read *perquiras. Requiris autem*
b G4   reads *sibi ipsi satisfacere* but R10Be VBP have
                             ipse
c G4 R10 Be   read *autem sibi ipsum potest* but BP omit *ipsum*
d G4 R10 Be V   P   read *et affectus noster bene sequendi, est*

26

a G4 R10 Be   read *superne ac procul*
b G4   reads *eminentia: statuasque* but punctuation
                             mark in R10 VBP is a full stop. Be unclear
                             at this point.
c G4   reads *eorum quae circumferuntur* and R10Be
                             read likewise but spell third word
                             circunferuntur
d G4 R10 Be   read *loqui opinarentur? Quod* but V has
                             opinantur: which BP follow.
e G4 R10 Be   read *Et si coegerit eum* but P reads *Etsi cogeret*
                             at the beginning.
f G4 R10   read *dum raptatur existimas?* but Be VBP have
                             raptetur which is preferred.
g G4 R10   V P   read *in regione simulachra* and Be likewise
                             except spelling last word *simulacra*
h G4 R10 Be   read *poterit. Animaduertit tandem*
i G4   V   read *tenebris obfundetur? Ac* and R10Be
                             likewise except for spelling of *offundetur* but
                             BP have *offendetur*
j G4 R10 Be   P   read *ipsis disceptare cum*
k G4 R10 Be   read *ipso in tempore* but VBP omit *in*
l G4 R10 Be   read *ad eam quae* and V reads likewise but the
                             line over the 'a' of *ea* is indistinct and was
                             presumably missed by those preparing B and
                             in turn therefore P.
m G4   reads *potentiam. Postremos in ascensum* but
                             middle two words in R10Be VBP read
                             Postremo si which are followed.

n G4 R10 Be	read *mente quicquam uel* but B has middle word *aliquid* which P copies.
o G4 R10 Be V P	read *neque mireris quod*
p G4 R10 Be	read *quippe id est, siquidem* and V reads likewise with middle words rendered thus *id ē* but for B these words were taken as *idem* which P repeats.
q G4 R10 Be	read *illis quarum umbrae*
r G4 R10 Be	read *miserebitur. Ac si* but VBP have *At* which is preferred.
s G4 R10 Be V P	read *a lumine superno*

27

a G4 R10 Be	read *uitam agat bestiae* although G4 has verb *agit* corrected to *agat* and VBP have *agit* which is followed.
b G4 R10	have in the margin opposite the address *Item locterio Neronio*. This indicates that a copy was sent to him as well. Be has the name *Locterio Neronio* in place of *Joanni Nesio* in the address.
c G4	has in the margin opposite the opening words of the body of the letter *Ratio Prima* and R10 has *Ratio 1*
d G4	has a paragraph mark at *Nihil prorsus* with the words *Ratio Secunda* in the margin. R10 has *Ratio 2*
e G4	has a paragraph mark at *Nullus usquam* and *Tertia* in the margin. R10 has *3*. VBP read *Nullus unquam*
f G4	has a paragraph mark at *Quandoque terrenis* and *Quarta* in the margin. R10 has *4*
g G4	has a paragraph mark at *Aut omnes* and *Quinta* in the margin. R10 has *5*
h G4	reads *patriaque quiescent*. R10Be VBP, however, have verb *quiescerent* which is preferred.
i G4 R10 Be V P	read *iusta prodesse, haec*
j G4 R10 Be V	read *pluribus capitibus redimitae*
k G4 R10 Be V P	read *protinus amputans: dum*
l G4 R10 Be	read *beniuolentia sibique conciliat* but VBP have *sibi*
m G4 R10 Be	read *neque ueri quicquam* but VBP omit *ueri*

n G4 R10   V   read *tanquam aurige parere. Sed* in which second word must be read as *aurigae*. Be P have this latter spelling.

o G4 R10 Be   read *imaginatione semouerit. Hic* but VBP have in the middle *se mouerit*.

p G4 R10 Be V   read *quaedam et illa*

q G4 R10 Be   read *multae, nil mirum esse* but VBP have *nimirum* instead of the two middle words.

28

a G4 R10 Be V   read *carissimo compatri suo*

b G4 R10 Be   read *quisque secumque omnia* but VBP have *secum*

c G4 R10 Be V   read *ipse raptus fuit* but BP have *captus*

d G4 R10 Be   read *reperit et seipsum*, but V has an abbreviation mark over *et* which indicates *etiam* and thus BP have this.

e G4 R10 Be V   P   read *seruus est et*

29

a G4 R10 Be V   read *amori, aut siqua*

b G4 R10   read *gratia disserimus contra fatum. 28 Junij 1477 Florentiae.* Be reads similarly but adds *Vale* after *fatum*. VB read as G4 except that they have verb *dixerimus* and omit month. P reads as V but gives month. P followed here.

30

a   Be V B P   read *Marsilius Ficinus Bernardo Bembo* and G4 reads likewise but omits *Bembo*. R10 reads as Be but has *florentinus* added after *Ficinus*. Be etc. followed here.

b G4 R10   read *Nulla arctior iocundior* and Be P read likewise but spell last word *iucundior*. V reads as G4 but has *actior* and B reads as V except for *iucundior*. The MSS spelling *arctior* is unusual, but, in our opinion, is intended to mean *actior*

31

a G4	reads *iam iam salutaueram, ipse* but R10Be VBP have the verb *salutaturam* which is preferred.
b G4 R10 Be V	read *scribo ad omnes*
c R10	after *amabo.* (which is the last word of letter 31) continues with the body of the next letter.

32

a G4 Be	read *conphilosophis suis, praecipue* but VBP omit *suis*
b G4 R10 Be V P	read *unionem aliquam esse*
c G4 R10 Be V P	read *inuident et*
d G4 R10 Be V P	read *quod et infinitum*
e G4 R10 Be V P	read *deum duobus praecipue*
f G4 R10 Be	read *omnem cogitationis. affectus. actionis nixum* but V has an abbreviation mark over the 'u' of *affectu* indicating *affectum*, which BP repeat.
g G4 R10 Be	read *hic solus dei*
h G4 R10 Be P	read *corporis speciosi picturam*
i G4 R10 Be B	read *mentes inextimabili quadam* but P has *inaestimabili*. The unusual spelling in MSS must be taken to imply P reading.
j G4 R10 Be V	read *et inuicem*
k G4 R10 Be V	read *deo unio uera*. BP, however, have *unico*

33

a G4 R10 Be V	read *inuidere non poteris*
b G4 R10 Be	read *cecam dicunt, quia* and in G4R10 the adjective must be read as *caecum*
c G4 R10 Be V P	read *subiecti uidentur, qui*

34

a G4 R10 V	read *saepe cum fenore* and Be reads likewise but spells the noun *foenore*
b G4 R10 Be V	read *sui uiuentem sculpit*
c G4 R10 Be V	read *qua gubernanda prudentiae*
d G4 R10 Be P	read *in affinium officio*

e G4 R10   B P   read *hymenea sacra musis* but Be has *sacris*
                            which reading is followed.

f G4 R10   P   read *sydera tollere uultus.* Be V read likewise
                            but spell first word *sidera*

g G4   reads *aequis pene* but R10Be BP have first
                            word *aequisque* which is followed.

h G4   reads *humanas transcendit. Hic* but R10Be V
                            have *transcendat*

i G4 R10 Be V   P   read *humani societatem, et*

j G4 R10 Be V   P   read *non fuerit occupatus*

k G4 R10 Be V B   read *amorem coniugis et*

l G4 R10 Be V B   read *is cui neque sit suis* but P reads *is qui
                            neque scit suis* which is followed.

m G4 R10 Be V   P   read *dignitates · caelestis reipublicae*

35

a G4 R10 Be V   P   read *Philosophia sapientiam gignit,*

b G4 R10   read *Marsilius Ficinus Sebastiano Saluino
                            amitino suo. s. d.* and V reads likewise except
                            third word *Bastiano.* B reads as V but omits
                            suo. P reads as G4 but omits *suo.* Be reads as
                            V but after *suo* has just *S.*

c G4 R10 Be   read *possumus ab illa quicquam* and V reads
                            similarly but puts words *ab illa* after *quicquam*
                            which order BP follow.

d G4 R10 Be V   P   read *apollinis iudicio sapientissimus.*

e G4 R10 Be   read *ille diuinus insipientibus* but BP have
                            middle word *sapientissimus*

f G4 R10 Be V   read *succedunt bene qui bene omnibus*

g   R10 Be V B P   read *qui soli uere* but G4 omits *soli.* R10etc.
                           followed.

h G4 R10   V B P   read *aliquid sapiant, maxime*

i G4 R10 Be V   P   read *Tunc Socratem diuinum*

36

a G4   reads *saemper morum elegantia* and R10Be VP
                           read likewise but spell first word *semper*

b G4 R10 Be V   P   read *dignior iudicaris, quanto*

c G4 R10 Be   read *suum clementior fuisse*

37

a G4		has the address *Marsilius ficinus Petro pannonio archepiscopo colocensi, uenerando in christo patri, litteratissimo litteratorum patrono plurimum se commendat.* In Be the address reads *Marsilius Ficinus Ioannifrancisco Hippolyto Gazolti comiti uiro clarissimo.* R10, after omitting entire heading, reads as Be but omits *Ioannifrancisco* and adds *S.D.* at end. VBP read as Be but have third word *Francisco* and add *S.D.* at end. Edd. followed.
b G4		read *mictam cum scriba* but R10 Be VBP in place of middle word have *cum primum* with Be VP spelling first word *mittam.* R10 followed.
c G4 R10 Be		read *huc et illuc impelluntur*
d G4 R10 Be V		read *quod raro et uix et obscure*
e	Be	reads *praenuntiant* and G4 R10 *prenumptiant* which must be taken to support Be reading but VBP have *pronunciant*
f	Be V B P	read *miseri fingimus, patimurque fingendo.* G4 reads likewise but has *fugimus* for first verb. R10 reads as G4 but has *fugiendo* for second verb. Be followed.
g	Be V B P	read *placet: ne cui forsan* but G4 R10 seem to join the middle two words, although the sense requires otherwise.
h G4 R10 Be V		read *enim fatum Marsilium* but BP omit *fatum* and VBP omit question-mark at end of sentence.
i G4 R10		read *uerum aliquid incidant. Sapere* but Be has *aliquod* and VBP have that and *incidunt*
j G4 R10 Be V		read *morbi praesagiunt. Ac*
k G4		read *ipsi tamen casu* although R10 has an abbreviation for *tamen.* It looks very much as if those preparing V mis-read this abbreviation for *inde* as that is the word V has, which BP follow. This points very strongly to V copying R10.
l G4	Be	read *tranquillitatisque pretiosissimae cupidi.*
m G4		reads *agite iam, accingite* but R10 Be V have no punctuation mark and BP have the comma before *iam* which is followed.
n G4 R10 Be V	P	read *defensione supercelesti deo*

o G4 R10 Be	read .*Tuum istud defendere imperium nunc aggredimur.* but V has full-stop after *imperium* and a colon at the end. BP have full-stop in middle as V, but commas at beginning and end.
p G4 R10 Be V P	read *suis non praestigijs*
q G4, Be	after *caelo.* have new paragraph: *Vale feliciter uenerande pater: atque Marsilium tuum inuicto pannoniae regi commenda. Petrumque garasdam et Dominicum iunium praeclaros uiros habeas commendatos.*

38

a G4	reads *Platonis. Ad* but R10Be have *,ad* and VBP follow R10 but omit comma. R10 followed.
b G4 R10 Be P	read *natali Plato* but VB have intervening full-stop.
c G4 R10 V	read *mars ille seuissimus* and Be P read likewise, except *saeuissimus*
d G4 R10 Be	read *potentia simul et* and V has abbreviated middle word which must be taken as *simul* but BP read *similiter*
e G4 R10	read *Qui diu platonis* and Be reads likewise but *qui* (more correctly). V reads as G4 and BP read as Be but *diui*. BP followed.
f G4 R10 Be V	read *inquam, Id est decus id est* but BP omit first *id est*

39

a G4 R10	read *non superant animos* but Be BP read as printed.
b G4 R10 Be	read *.Fieri uero nequit ab* and V reads likewise but omits the stop and adds *ut* after *nequit*. V followed (as grammatically correct) but with a full-stop.
c Be	reads *mecum inuitis* but G4R10 V have intervening full-stop and capital. BP have comma. Be BP followed.
d G4 R10 Be V B	read *VIII Kalendas Junias MCCCCLXXVIIII. Florentiae.*

Notes on Ficino's Correspondents
and other Contemporaries mentioned in this Volume

Details are given below of correspondents and contemporaries about whom significant details are known to the translators. The following abbreviations used in the notes are here given in full:

Cosenza—M. E. Cosenza, *Biographical Dictionary of Humanism and Classical Scholarship*, 5 vols., Boston, 1962.

Della Torre—A. Della Torre, *Storia dell'Accademia Platonica di Firenze*.

Diz. Biog. Ital.—*Dizionario Biografico degli Italiani*, Rome, 1960 onwards.

Iter Ital.—P. O. Kristeller, *Iter Italicum*, a finding list of uncatalogued or incompletely catalogued humanistic manuscripts of the Renaissance in Italian and other libraries, 2 vols., London and Leiden, 1963, 1967 onwards.

Kristeller, *Studies*—P. O. Kristeller, *Studies in Renaissance Thought and Letters*.

Marcel—R. Marcel, *Marsile Ficin*.

Sup. Fic.—P. O. Kristeller, *Supplementum Ficinianum*.

Vespasiano—Vespasiano da Bisticci, *Lives of illustrious Men of the XVth Century*, translated by W. George & E. Waters, introduction by Myron P. Gillmore.

Marcello Virgilio Adriani (1464–1521): Professor of Greek and Latin at Florence University from 1497 and Chancellor of Florence from 1498 to 1521. As Chancellor he wrote the funeral oration for Ficino and Alamanno Rinuccini. He translated from the Greek and wrote a commentary on Dioscorides' *De Materia Medica*, a MS of which was first discovered in 1518. His other works include a Commentary on the first three books of the *Iliad* and *Lessons on the Education of the Florentine Nobility*. He was the colleague of Niccolo Machiavelli in the chancellery of Florence.

Sandys, *A History of Classical Scholarship*, Vol. 2, Cambridge, 1903, p. 135; Cosenza, pp. 58–9.

Riccardo Angiolieri of Anghiari (1414–1486): priest and member of the Florentine College of Theologians. He studied theology at Padua and Venice and lectured on the *Sentences* of Peter Lombard. Ficino sent him a number of philosophical letters, including one on the allegory of the cave from Plato's *Republic* (see letter 26).

Della Torre, p. 770 *seq*; Cosenza, pp. 184–5.

Giovanni Aurelio Augurelli of Rimini (1440–1524): poet and man of letters, Augurelli sent his poetry to Ficino who sang it to the accompaniment of his lyre. Augurelli also corresponded with Bembo and Poliziano. His Latin poetry, *Carmina*, was edited by Aldus Manutius (Venice, 1505). He also wrote the *Chrysopoeiae*, an allegorical poem on alchemy dedicated to Pope Leo X (Venice 1515), for which the Pope rewarded him with an empty purse.

Della Torre, pp. 818–19; *Sup. Fic.*, II, p. 336; *Diz. Biog. Ital.*, *Vol. 4, pp.* 578–81 (full bibliography).

Marco Aurelio of Venice: scholar who held public office. He was Secretary to the Venetian Senate (*Secretario Ducale*), and succeeded Giovanni Pietro Stella as Grand Chancellor of Venice. He went on an embassy to the Turks. Ficino sent him a letter in praise of philosophy and one in praise of medicine (*Opera*, pp. 757, 759; see also letters 13 and 14). Many letters from Filelfo are addressed to him. He also corresponded with Giuliano de' Medici, Bernardo Bembo, Guarino and Nicolo Sagundino.

Sup. Fic., I, p. 119; Cosenza, p. 336; *Iter Ital.*, II.

Francesco Bandini (*c.* 1440–1489): priest and diplomatic agent, who was sent on various missions by the Medici. He was a close friend of Ficino and a member of the Platonic Academy. He was appointed Master of the Wine Cup (*architryclinus*) at the Platonic Symposium described by Ficino in *De Amore*. Ficino dedicated his *Life of Plato* (letter 19) to Bandini. After a sojourn at the court of King Ferrante of Naples, Bandini was sent to the court of King Matthias of Hungary in 1476 and remained there for the rest of his life, continuing to correspond with Ficino and Lorenzo de'Medici (although his brother, Bernardo Bandini, was a conspirator in the Pazzi plot and struck the blow which killed Giuliano de' Medici). In Buda Francesco founded the *Coetus*, a circle of humanists, and numbered among his friends Bartolomeo della Fonte and Ugolino Verino. His correspondence is preserved in the State Archives of Florence.

Della Torre, p. 768 *seq.*; *Sup. Fic.*, I, p. 121; Kristeller, *Studies*, pp. 395–435 *et passim*; Cosenza, pp. 388–9; *Diz. Biog. Ital.*, Vol. 5, pp. 709–10.

Ermolao Barbaro (1454–1493): distinguished Venetian humanist and diplomat. He followed his father in a diplomatic career early in life, although drawn to literary pursuits. In 1468 he was crowned Poet Laureate by the Emperor Frederick III, in Verona. For a while he was a member of the *Maggior Consilio* of the Venetian Republic and became a Senator in 1483. Later he was Ambassador at Milan and Rome. Pope Innocent VIII appointed him Patriarch of Aquila in 1491, which position he accepted without the permission of Venice, although Venetian law forbade her ambassadors to accept offices from foreign sovereigns without first obtaining the consent of the Venetian Senate. The Council of Ten commanded Ermolao to relinquish the position or be deprived of office and property. The Pope, to assert his own authority, threatened Barbaro with excommunication if he resigned. Barbaro preferred to obey the Pope and spent the last years of his life an exile in Rome.

Ermolao corresponded with Ficino, who sent him a copy of *De Vita Libri Tres* on publication (1489). Ficino enlisted his aid concerning the charge of magic brought against his *De Vita*; Ermolao persuaded Pope Innocent VIII to decide in Ficino's favour (see letter from Ermolao in *Opera*, I, p. 912). Apart from a few writings on Aristotle, he wrote a work on the office of ambassador, *De Officio Legati*, and another on celibacy, *De Coelibatu*. Several of Barbaro's letters and orations are printed at the end of Poliziano's *Epistolae Libri XII*, Antwerp.

Vittore Branca, *E. Barbaro, Epistolae, Orationes, Carmina*, Florence, 1943; *Diz. Biog. Ital.*, Vol. 6, pp. 96–9; Cosenza, pp. 404–12, *Sup. Fic.*, II, 336.

Nicolaus Bathory: Bishop of Vacz, humanist who acted as a counsellor to King Matthias of Hungary. He corresponded with Ficino and tried to persuade him to come to the Hungarian court. He also corresponded with Sebastiano Salvini.

Della Torre, p. 93, 100; Kristeller, *Studies*, p. 376.

Bernardo Bembo (1433–1519): Venetian ambassador and statesman, father of Pietro Bembo. He was appointed Venetian Ambassador to Florence in 1474; the friend of Lorenzo, Poliziano and Ficino, who dedicated the fifth book of the *Letters* to him. In Florence Bembo's platonic love for Ginevra de' Benci was celebrated in numerous poems of Braccesi. In Venice Bembo frequented the literary circle of Aldus Manutius.

Della Torre, 'La prima ambasceria di Bernardo Bembo a Firenze' in *Giornale Storico*, XXXV (1900), p. 258 *seq*; *Sup. Fic.*, II, p. 346; Cosenza, pp. 489–90; *Diz. Biog. Ital.*, Vol. 8, p. 103 *seq*.

Francesco Berlinghieri (1440–1501): Florentine patrician, poet and geographer. He held many offices, including that of *Priore* and *Gonfaloniere di Compagnia* (1478), and went on various missions. At the age of 25 he translated Ptolemy's *Geography* into *terza rima*. It had an introduction by Ficino and was dedicated to Federico, Duke of Urbino. Ficino sent Berlinghieri his oracular letter '*Spiritus ubi vult spirat*' (*Opera*, p. 812) and dedicated Book VII of the *Epistolae* to him. Together with Filippo Valori, Francesco helped to bring out a sumptuous edition of Ficino's Latin version of Plato (1484). Ficino praises Berlinghieri in his commentary on Plato's *Timaeus* (*Opera*, p. 1464 *seq*.).

Diz. Biog. Ital., Vol. 9, p. 121 *seq*. (full bibliography); Della Torre, pp. 666–7; *Sup. Fic.*, II, 326; A. Mori, 'Un Geografo del Rinascimento, F. Berlinghieri' in *Archivio Storico Italiano*, XIII (1894), p. 341 *seq*.

Jacopo Bracciolini (1441–1478): son of Poggio, the famous humanist. A scholar, member of Ficino's Academy and secretary to Cardinal Raffaele Riario (1477). He took part in the Pazzi conspiracy against the Medici and was hanged. Ficino's letter to Jacopo, quoting an epistle from Plutarch to Trajan, was written shortly before the conspiracy. An earlier letter of Ficino's in praise of history is also addressed to Jacopo (see *Letters*, Vol. 1, letter 107).

Jacopo's works include an Italian translation of his father's *Historia Fiorentina* as well as translations of various classical works, including the 'Lives of the Two Antonines' from *Scriptores Historiae Augustae*. He also wrote (in Italian) *On the Origins of the War between the English and French*, which is based on a Latin novel by Bartolomeo Fazio. Ironically, he addressed a *Declamatio Contra Detractores* to Lorenzo de' Medici.

Iter Ital., I. pp. 124, 126; Cosenza, pp. 693–4; *Diz. Biog. Ital.*, Vol. 13, pp. 638–9 (full bibliography); see also A. Poliziano, *Della Congiura dei Pazzi*, ed. A. Perosa, Padova, 1958.

Lorenzo Buonincontri of San Miniato (1411–1492): philosopher, astronomer and poet. He was a member of Ficino's Academy and a close friend of Lorenzo de' Medici. Ficino sought Buonincontri's advice on questions of astronomy. Buonincontri wrote many works on philosophy and astronomy, including an important commentary on Manilius's *Astronomicon* and a poem 'Atlante' in *ottava rima*. He was also a soldier of fortune, and served in the army of Costanzo Sforza.

Della Torre, pp. 681–7; Thorndike, *History of Magic and Experimental Science*, IV, p. 405 *seq.*; Cosenza, p. 659 *seq.*

Giovanni Canacci: Florentine aristocrat who held public office. He was a member of the *Dieci di Liberta* (1498) and one of the *Dodici Buonomini* when Savonarola, whom he opposed, was condemned. He belonged to Ficino's Academy and later to the *Orti Oricellari*. Ficino asked Canacci, as well as Ermolao Barbaro and Amerigo Corsini, to defend him against a charge of heresy over his *De Vita Libri Tres*.

Della Torre, p. 732; *Sup. Fic.*, I, p. 129.

Febo Capella: Venetian humanist. For many years he was scribe or *cancellarius* to the Venetian Republic and was made Grand Chancellor in 1480. In 1463 he went on a mission to Florence. Ficino dedicated his *Quid Sit Lumen* (*Opera*, p. 717) to Capella. Febo also corresponded with Sagundino, Filelfo and Francesco Barbaro. Naldo Naldi wrote verses to him.

Giovanni Cavalcanti (1444–1509): son of a Florentine nobleman, he studied rhetoric under Landino and became a statesman and diplomat, going on an important mission to King Charles VIII of France in 1494. Ficino knew and loved Giovanni from the time when Giovanni was only three years old. Ficino dedicated his translations of Alcinous and Speusippus to him in 1463 (see Vol. I, letter 51). In Cavalcanti's company Ficino wrote many of his works, such as the *Platonic Theo-*

logy. Cavalcanti remained devoted to Ficino all his life. When Ficino was afflicted with a 'bitterness of spirit' (Corsi VIII, see p. 139), Cavalcanti advised him to write a book on love as a remedy for his illness and to 'convert the lovers of transitory beauty to the enjoyment of eternal beauty'. This work became the first version of *De Amore*, the commentary on Plato's *Symposium* which is dedicated to Cavalcanti. He should not be confused with the famous Florentine historian Giovanni Cavalcanti (1381–1451) who wrote the *Istorie Fiorentine*.

Della Torre, p. 647 *seq.* & index; *Sup. Fic.*, I, p. 118; Marcel, pp. 340–6 & index; Cosenza, pp. 951–3

Giovanni Corsi (1472–1547): Florentine statesman. He was a leading member of the Medici party, who opposed the government of Piero Soderini. After the return of the Medici in 1512 he held the highest offices of state, being *Gonfaloniere di Giustizia* and a member of the Senate from 1512. Corsi frequented the *Orti Oricellari* and was a close friend of Bernardo Rucellai. Apart from his *Life of Ficino*, written during the exile of the Medici in 1506, Corsi made translations from Plutarch and edited Pontano's *De Prudentia*. Corsi's teacher was Francesco da Diacceto, whose *Panegyricus in Amorem* is dedicated to him see Notes on Corsi's *Life of Marsilio Ficino*, p. 153, note 56).

'Un Uomo di Stato e Umanista Fiorentino, Giovanni Corsi' in Kristeller, *Studies*, p. 175 *seq.*; see also 'Per la Biografia di Marsilio Ficino', *ibid*, p. 191 *seq.*; Marcel, pp. 15–26; Della Torre, pp. 42–4.

Matthias Corvinus: King of Hungary from 1458 to 1490. His real name was Hunyadi, but he was surnamed 'Corvinus' from the raven (*corvus*) on his escutcheon. He was one of Hungary's greatest monarchs, long honoured as a national hero. Within three years of his accession, in the face of strong opposition both from within his own country and from the Holy Roman Emperor, he succeeded in establishing himself firmly on the throne. From 1461 he was engaged in a long struggle against the Turks. His most notable victories over the Sultan were won in 1480–81, when he drove the Turks out of Servia as well as assisting in their defeat at Otranto (see Vol. 2, letter 1 and note). In 1485 after defeating the German emperor Frederick III, he made a triumphal entry into Vienna which for a time became his capital.

Matthias was a true monarch of the Renaissance, at once gifted as a soldier, statesman, legislator and patron of the arts and humanities. His capacity for work was apparently inexhaustible: frequently he would spend half the night in reading after the labour of the most strenuous day. There was no branch of learning in which he did not take a keen interest. He established a university in Buda (Budapest) and founded a library, the 'Corvina', in which he planned to collect the works of all classical authors. He was a great patron of the fine arts, especially miniature illumination. He gave commissions to such artists as Benedetto da Maiano, Filippino Lippi and Andrea del Verrochio. The palace he built at Buda was pronounced to be the equal of any in Italy.

Marsilio Ficino was invited to teach at Buda but declined. However, Bartolomeo della Fonte and other scholars from the Platonic Academy lived at Buda for some years. Francesco Bandini, also a member of Ficino's Academy, accompanied Beatrice of Aragon to Hungary when she married King Matthias in 1476. In addition to the third and fourth books of his *Letters*, Ficino also dedicated the third book of *De Vita Libri Tres* to the King. The King corresponded with Lorenzo de' Medici, whom he admired, and offered to mediate between Lorenzo and Pope Sixtus IV during the wars that followed the Pazzi conspiracy.

Cosenza, pp. 1124–5; Kristeller, *Studies*, pp. 395–401, 411–5.

Francesco Cattani da Diacceto (1466–1522): distinguished Florentine humanist and philosopher. Diacceto was one of Ficino's leading disciples, and after Ficino's death came to be regarded as his successor because of his dedication to the task of spreading Plato's philosophy. He studied philosophy under the Aristotelian Oliviero Arduini, and taught at Florence University, where he held the Chair of Moral Philosophy. Diacceto frequented the *Orti Oricellari* and was also a member of the *Academia Sacra Fiorentina* (1515–19), which regarded itself as a revival of the Platonic Academy, and included Michelangelo among its members. After the downfall of Piero Soderini, Diacceto held important public offices and became *Gonfaloniere* in 1520. He died shortly before the discovery of a plot involving some of his pupils.

His writings comprise the *Panegirico all' Amore* and *I Tre Libri dello Amore* a treatise on love first written in Latin as *De Amore*. His most famous work, the *De Pulchro* (On the Beautiful), reflects some ideas of Plotinus. Like Pico della Mirandola, he intended to write a work on the harmony or agreement between Plato and Aristotle. Diacceto also corresponded with leading churchmen and statesmen, including Cardinal Domenico Grimani, Pope Leo X and the French humanist Germain de Ganay.

The *Life of Diacceto* by Benedetto Varchi (in Italian) was printed in 1561 together with his two vernacular treatises on Love. His Latin works were published in *Opera Omnia Francisci Catanei Diaccetii*, Basle, 1563, with a biography by Frosino Lapini.

P. O. Kristeller, 'Francesco da Diacceto and Florentine Platonism in the 16th Century', in *Studies*, p. 287 *seq.*

Francesco d'Este (1433–1478): illegitimate son of Lionello d'Este, Marquis of Ferrara. In 1444 he was sent to the Burgundian court to be educated with the young Charles the Bold. He spent most of his life in the Netherlands where he held various military offices. He returned to Italy on several occasions, as an Ambassador of Burgundy. His portrait was painted by Rogier van der Weyden (Metropolitan Museum).

Nicholas of Euboea or **Nicolo Sagundino of Negroponte (Euboea)**: came to Italy with his family in 1438. Being fluent in Greek and Latin he acted as an interpreter at the Council of Florence. He later settled in Venice and became a citizen of the Republic, going on various embassies. He translated certain works of Demosthenes (*Orations*) and other classical authors from Greek into Latin, and corresponded with leading humanists such as Andronicos Callistus, Bessarion and Theodore of Gaza. Writings and letters of Nicolo Sagundino are preserved in a Vatican MS *Ottob. Lat.* 1732, including a dialogue on Plato and Aristotle between Nicolo, Febo Capella and Marco Aurelio.

Legrand, *Bibliographie Hellénique*; *Iter Ital.*, II, p. 432 *et passim.*

Pope Eugene IV (1383–1447): Gabriele Condulman of Venice, elected Pope in 1431.

Bartolomeo della Fonte (1445–1513): Florentine priest, poet, and orator. He succeeded Francesco Filelfo (died 1481) as Professor of Rhetoric and Philosophy at Florence University, but was forced to resign because of the hostility of Poliziano. After teaching in Rome, he regained his position in 1485 with the help of Lorenzo de' Medici. For a time he taught at the court of King Matthias of Hungary, whose library he helped to enrich. He returned to Florence in 1490 on the death of the King. *Opera* published in Frankfurt, 1621.

Della Torre, p. 420 *seq.*; C. Marchesi, *Bartolomeo della Fonte*, Catania, 1900; *Epistolae*, ed. J. Fogel and L. Juhasz, Leipzig, 1932; Cosenza, pp. 1448–53; *Epistolae*, ed. L. Juhasz, Budapest, 1931.

Lorenzo Franceschi: scholar who made an Italian translation of six dialogues of Plato from Ficino's Latin translation, and an Italian translation of Ficino's Life of Plato.

Iter Ital., I, p. 114.

Jacopo Guicciardini (1422–1490): Florentine statesman, son of Piero Guicciardini. He was *Priore, Gonfaloniere di Giustizia* and *Commissarius Generalis* of the Florentine army against Volterra in 1472, and in the war of the Pazzi conspiracy (1478–9). Jacopo wrote the *Ricordi* (*Memoirs*). Ficino dedicated his *Sermoni Morali della Stultitia et Miseria degli Uomini* to Jacopo in 1478. His letters are preserved in the State Archives of Florence.

Litta, *Le Famiglie Celebri Italiane*, Vol. III; F. Guicciardini, *Opere Inedite*, ed. Canestrini, Vol. 10, Florence, 1867.

Piero di Jacopo Guicciardini (1454–1513): Son of Jacopo and father of Francesco, the celebrated historian. A statesman who held important offices, including that of *Priore*. In Francesco's dialogue *Del Reggimento di Firenze Libri Due*, Piero is described as discussing with Ficino the three forms of government, monarchy, oligarchy and democracy. Piero was one of three friends to whom Ficino addressed his *Apologia*

(September 1489) defending himself against charges of heresy over his *De Vita Libri Tres* (see *Opera* pp. 572–4).

    F. Guicciardini, *Opere Inedite*, ed. Canestrini, Vol. 10, Florence, 1867; *Sup. Fic.*, II, p. 344; Cosenza, p. 1733.

Giovanni Francesco Ippoliti, Count of Gazzoldo: humanist, and friend of Ficino. In 1480 Francesco caused the first six books of Ficino's *Epistolae* to be transcribed. Ficino addressed a long letter (letter 18) to Francesco on the platonic nature and function of a philosopher. Letters by him are preserved in the Archivio Mediceo avanti il Principato.

Antonio Ivani of Sarzana (*c.* 1430–1482): scholar who held public offices. He was Chancellor of Volterra (1466–71) and Pistoia. He wrote a book on the sack of Volterra as well as a book in Italian on the family, *Del Governo della Famiglia* (ed. Bertoloni, Genova, 1872). His correspondents included Ficino and Donato Acciaiuoli. His unpublished letters are preserved in Sarzana (cod. Sarzan., xxvi).

    Sup. Fic., II, p. 324; *Iter Ital.*, pp. 144–5.

Cristoforo Landino (1424–1504): Florentine poet, scholar and humanist, and member of Ficino's Academy. He shared with Ficino the duties of instructing the young Lorenzo. From 1458 he was Professor of Poetry and Rhetoric at Florence University, and Secretary to the Signoria until 1492. All his life Landino encouraged the study of the three great poets of Florence—Dante, Petrarch and Boccaccio. In 1481 he published an edition of the *Divine Comedy* with a commentary, and illustrations by Botticelli. He also wrote commentaries on Horace and Virgil which influenced poets and artists. Landino's most famous Latin work is the *Camaldolese Dialogues* of 1475 (see Vol. I, letter 119). Ficino dedicated his *Institutiones ad Platonicam Disciplinam* to Landino. Landino expounded the speech of Aristophanes at the Platonic banquet held on 7th November, 1468 (described by Ficino in his Commentary on Plato's *Symposium*). His friends included Alberti and Bembo, and his pupils the Englishmen, William Grocyn and Thomas Linacre.

    Della Torre, pp. 380 *seq.*, 579; *Sup. Fic.*, II, pp. 327–8; Marcel, p. 190 *seq.* & index; Cosenza, pp. 1909–16; *Carmina Omnia*, ed. A. Perosa, 1939; *De Vera Nobilitate*, ed. M. T. Liaci, Florence, 1970; *De Vera Nobilitate*, ed. M. Lentzen, Geneva, 1970; *De Nobilitate Animae*, ed. C. Paoli and G. Gentile in *Annali delle Università Toscane* 34–36 (1915–17).

Jacopo Lanfredini: father of Antonio. Statesman and diplomat who held important offices in the Republic; he was one of the *Priori* in 1460 and 1471, and *Gonfaloniere* in 1477. He was also twice envoy to Duke Ercole d'Este and later envoy to Pope Sixtus IV (1480). He corresponded with Ficino (see *Opera*, p. 835–6).

Pier Leone (Pietro Leoni) of Spoleto (d. 1492): physician and astrologer, learned in Greek and Latin. He lectured on Manilius' *Astronomicon* at Florence University (1476–8). He was twice professor of medicine at Pisa University and also lectured at Rome and Padua. He was a close friend of Lorenzo de' Medici and was the physician in attendance on Lorenzo during his last illness. After Lorenzo's death in 1492, he was accused of misdiagnosing his illness and apparently committed suicide by throwing himself down a well, although murder was also suspected.

He was a close disciple of Ficino and member of the Platonic Academy. Ficino sent him a copy of *De Vita Libri Tres* and his commentary on Plotinus. Pier Leone asked Ficino to translate the *Aphorisms* of Hippocrates; Ficino declined and they were later translated by Poliziano. He possessed a fine library of Greek and Latin texts.

L. Dorez, 'Recherches sur la bibliothèque de Pier Leoni, Medecin de Laurent de' Medicis' in *Revue des Bibliothèques*, VII (1897), pp. 80–106; *ibid*, IV (1894), pp. 73–83. On his death—see L. Frati, 'La morte di Lorenzo de' Medici e il suicidio di Pier Leoni', in *Rinascimento*, 6, p. 333, and *Archivio Storico Italiano*, Ser. 5, Vol. 4 (1889), p. 255 *seq.*; Della Torre, pp. 785–7; *Sup. Fic.*, I p. 123; Consenza, pp. 2782–3.

Francesco Marescalchi of Ferrara (d. 1482): canon and member of Ficino's Academy. Ficino addressed the preface to his work on astrology to Francesco, as well as dedicating the *De Christiana Religione* to him. He was a pupil of Guarino of Verona and he corresponded with Poggio Bracciolini. For this correspondence see P. Gordan, *Two Renaissance Book Hunters*, New York, 1974 (notes to letter 1, pp. 215–20). His *Carmina* is preserved in the Marciana Library, Venice (cod. Lat., XII, 91, [4123]).

Della Torre, p. 600; Cosenza, pp. 1484–5.

Cosimo de' Medici (1389–1464): statesman, banker, scholar, and patron of the arts. Cosimo as a man towers above the many functions which he so ably performed. At the death of his father he was possessed of a vast fortune and wide experience both in commerce and diplomacy. Of gentle and kind manners, and immensely generous, he was also blessed with the widest vision and a spirit of philanthropy that deployed his resources with remarkable effectiveness. He was particularly generous towards artists and scholars.

From 1429 Cosimo was head of a great banking house with interests all over Europe and the Orient; from 1433 an active and devoted collector of ancient manuscripts; and from 1434, the first citizen of Florence. Inspired by Gemistos Plethon with renewed enthusiasm for the study of Plato, Cosimo determined to establish a new Platonic Academy in Florence. To lead the Academy he chose Marsilio Ficino, entrusting him in 1462 with the translation and interpretation of the Platonic dialogues. Two years later, as he lay dying, Cosimo heard Ficino read to him the words of Xenocrates, a disciple of Plato, on the consolation of death.

128 THE LETTERS OF MARSILIO FICINO

Thus, at the age of seventy-five, died a man exemplary in private and public affairs, honoured as *Pater Patriae*.

A. Fabroni, *Magni Cosmi Medicei Vita*, Pisa, 1789; Della Torre, p. 559 *seq.* & index; C. S. Gutkind, *Cosimo de' Medici, Pater Patriae*, Oxford, 1940; Alison Brown, 'The Humanist Portrait of Cosimo de' Medici, Pater Patriae' in *Journal of the Warburg and Courtauld Institute*, 24, 1961, pp. 186–221; Marcel, pp. 255–62 & index. See also bibliography.

Lorenzo de' Medici (1449–1492): grandson of Cosimo and son of Piero. Lorenzo was one of the most versatile and talented men of his time: perhaps the finest Italian poet of the century, he was equally accomplished in philosophic and religious poetry, love poetry and comic poetry. An eminent statesman, his principles, particularly his respect for justice, arose from his love of religion and philosophy. Ficino, his boyhood tutor, he always regarded as a close friend. Their friendship appears to have been strongest at the time the letters in Book I were written.

He was only 21 when he found himself the effective ruler of Florence. He was faced with enemies both in Florence and outside. The most critical period of his rule was that of the Pazzi conspiracy (1478) in which his brother Giuliano was assassinated in Florence Cathedral and he only narrowly escaped. After the conspiracy he was opposed in war by a powerful alliance of Italian states under the leadership of the Pope, a war which his courage and statesmanship brought to a satisfactory conclusion. After this, through his statesmanship and the respect in which he was held, Italy enjoyed a period of comparative peace until his death.

From his love of knowledge and the arts Lorenzo revitalized the University of Pisa, discerned the latent talent in Michelangelo, and supported that group of artists, sculptors, poets, scholars and philosophers who were close to the heart of the Renaissance.

A. Fabroni, *Laurentii Medicis magnifici vita*, Pisa, 1784; A. Von Reumont, *Lorenzo de' Medici*, Leipzig, 1883, and London, 1876; see the new edition of the letters of Lorenzo de' Medici edited by N. Rubinstein, Florence, 1977, in progress; Della Torre, pp. 737–42 & index; Marcel, p. 372 *seq.* & index; Cosenza, pp. 2272–5. See also bibliography at the end of this volume.

Piero di Cosimo de' Medici (1416–1469): together with Cosimo his father, he was instrumental in inviting Argyropoulos to Florence in 1456 to teach Greek. He succeeded Cosimo as head of the Republic in 1464. Esteemed highly by many humanists, including Ficino, for his patronage of letters, he was a member of the *Chorus Achademiae Florentinae* (an Aristotelian School under Argyropoulos) and an *Officialis* of the Florentine *Studio* (University). Ficino dedicated to Piero his translation of three dialogues of Plato, *Hippias Maior*, *Lysis* and *Theaetetus*, as well as his translation of Xenocrates' *De Morte*.

Pico della Mirandola, Count of Concordia (1463–1494): humanist and philosopher, one of the foremost figures of the Renaissance. From an early age his learning was prodigious. He attended some of the leading universities of Italy and France over a period of seven years. In 1484, on a visit to Florence, he joined Ficino's Academy. Ficino praised Pico for his deep understanding of platonic philosophy and it was Pico who first advised Ficino to translate Plotinus. In 1484, during a stay at the Sorbornne in Paris, Pico conceived the idea of writing a polemic thesis 'On all knowledge' which became the *Nine Hundred Conclusions*. The work was published in 1486 but a papal commission declared thirteen theses to be heretical or suspect and the disputation was prohibited by Pope Innocent VIII. Pico fled to Paris, where he was imprisoned. Through the offices of Lorenzo de' Medici and King Charles VIII of France he was pardoned and allowed to settle in Florence, devoting the remaining years of his life to theology and philosophy. He studied Hebrew, Chaldaic and Arabic and was the first Western scholar to acquire a knowledge of Jewish Cabala, which he tried to harmonise with Christian theology. Pico's most famous work, the *Oration (On the Dignity of Man)*, emphasizes man's freedom to choose his own destiny. He began work on a Concordance between Plato and Aristotle but completed only the first part, the *De Ente et Uno*. He also wrote a major work against astrology. Pico began following the teachings of Savonarola in the monastery of San Marco and thought of becoming a Dominican but died on 17th November, 1494 (at the age of 31), the same day that King Charles VIII entered Florence.

The great personal appeal of the man, his precocious learning and early death have made his life into something of a legend. Machiavelli wrote in his *Histories* that Pico was 'almost divine'. His nephew, Giovanni Francesco Pico, wrote his life.

Pico's works were first published in Bologna in 1496, then in Venice in 1498. The 1572 Basle edition *Opera quae Extant Omnia* is the most complete, and includes his biography by Giovanni Francesco.

Pico della Mirandola, *De Hominis Dignitate*; ed. E. Garin (1942); *Disputationes Adversus Astrologiam*, ed. E. Garin, Florence, 1946–52; E. Garin, *Giovanni Pico della Mirandola*, Florence, 1937; *L'Opera e il Pensiero di Giovanni Pico della Mirandola*, Convegno Internazionale, Mirandola, 1963, Florence, 1965, which include articles on Pico by Kristeller and Frances Yates (on his sources and magic).

Lotterio Neroni: Florentine humanist of noble family, exiled in 1466 after being involved in a conspiracy against Piero de' Medici. He returned to Florence but held no public office. Friend of Ficino, Platina and the poet Ugolino Verino, he compiled excerpts from Cicero's letters. Ficino wrote an important letter on the soul to him, *Anima in corpore dormit, somniat, delirat, aegrotat* (*Opera Omnia*, p. 926).
Sup. Fic., I, p. 120; Cosenza, p. 2430.

Giovanni Nesi (1456–1520): poet, philosopher and faithful disciple of Ficino. He held public office, was three times *Priore* and an *Officialis* of the *Studio* (University). His writings comprise poems, letters and devotional orations, many of which were recited before the *Compagnia dei Magi*, a lay confraternity. He wrote a long visionary poem about Paradise, neoplatonic in style. Nesi also frequented the Convent of San Marco and followed the teaching of Savonarola, whom he praises in his *Oraculum de Novo Seculo* (1496). He had a deep admiration for Pico della Mirandola and corresponded with other poets: Poliziano, Naldi and della Fonte.

Della Torre, pp. 692–701; Cosenza, pp. 2432–3; C. Vasoli, 'Giovanni Nesi tra Donato Acciaiuoli e Girolamo Savonarola' in *Umanesimo e Teologia tra 400 e 500*, *Memorie Domenicane*, 4(1973).

Rinaldo Orsini: Archbishop of Florence and brother-in-law of Lorenzo, who was married to his sister Clarice Orsini. When Francesco Salviati tried to obtain the archbishopric of Florence on the death of Cardinal Pietro Riario in 1474, Lorenzo bestowed it on Rinaldo instead. In June 1490 Ficino appealed to Rinaldo for help against a charge of heresy directed against him at Rome in connection with his book on medicine and astrology, the *De Vita Libri Tres*. Rinaldo interceded in person on his behalf before Pope Innocent VIII and the charge was dropped.

Della Torre, p. 625; Cosenza, p. 3530.

Girolamo Pasqualini: scholar who possibly translated into Italian the passage from Marsuppini's *Rerum Sui Tempore Gestarum*, which describes the Aristotelian School of Manuel Chrysoloras, the Greek scholar invited in 1396 to teach at Florence, and the progress of some of the School's pupils.

Cosenza, p. 2620.

Cosimo Pazzi (1466–1513): Bishop of Arezzo and later of Florence (1508–1513). A nephew of Lorenzo de' Medici. He corresponded with leading humanists, including Ficino, Pope Pius III (Cardinal of Sienna) and Pope Julius II. He translated the platonic discourses of Maximus of Tyre into Latin.

Cosenza, p. 2529–30.

Antonio Pelotti: poet, and friend of the Medici. He corresponded with Ficino, who sent him a letter in praise of matrimony (letter 34). His extant writings include Italian sonnets and Latin epigrams.

Della Torre, p. 659 *seq*; Cosenza, p. 2660.

Platina (Bartolomeo Sacchi of Piadena) (1421–1481): distinguished scholar and humanist. He studied Greek under Argyropoulos for five years and became a close friend of Cosimo and Piero de' Medici. His dialogue *De Optimo Cive* (1474) describes conversations on statecraft held between himself, Cosimo and the young Lorenzo at Careggi. In Rome he became an Apostolic Abbreviator (papal secretary) under Pope Paul II. Later the Pope discharged all the abbreviators and imprisoned Platina when he protested. He became a member of the Roman Academy of

Pomponius Laetus but when this society was condemned by the Pope as being pagan and subversive, Platina was again imprisoned for one year. Pope Sixtus IV restored him to papal favour, making him Librarian of the Vatican in 1475. Platina died in the plague of 1481. His writings include *Lives of the Popes up to the Pontificate of Sixtus IV*, *De Falso et Vero Bono*, *De Vera Voluptate*. According to Corsi, Platina is said to have assisted Ficino in his study of Greek.

Platina, *De Optimo Cive*, ed. F. Battaglia, Bologna 1940; Della Torre, p. 531 *seq*; Cosenza, pp. 2839–46.

Georgios Gemistos Plethon (*c.* 1356–1452): Celebrated Greek philosopher and reformer and one of the chief pioneers of the revival of learning. His vision of a rebirth of Hellenism through a system of religious and social reform remained unfulfilled but he is chiefly remembered for introducing Plato to the West in a series of lectures delivered during the Council of Florence in 1439, which are said to have inspired Cosimo with the idea of founding a Platonic Academy. Plethon's proposed reform of Greek law and religion is set forth in the *Nomoi* or *Laws*, his most important work which is only partly extant. His other works include a *Compendium of the Teachings of Zoroaster and Plato* (The Chaldaeic oracles were first attributed to Zoroaster by Plethon). His belief in an 'ancient theology' or philosophical tradition beginning with Zoroaster, Orpheus and Hermes Trismegistus inspired Ficino's doctrine of *prisca theologia*, and Ficino calls Plethon *alter Plato* (the second Plato) in his proem to Plotinus (*Opera*, p. 1537).

Plethon, *Traité des Lois*, ed. C. Alexandre, Paris, 1858 (text and French translation of the *Nomoi*); F. Masai, *Plethon et le Platonisme de Mistra*, Paris, 1956; Della Torre, p. 428 *seq.*; Marcel, p. 133 *seq.*; Cosenza, pp. 2848–53.

Bindaccio Ricasoli (*c.* 1444–1524): Florentine aristocrat who held minor offices. He was a disciple of Ficino and later a member of the *Orti Oricellari*. Ficino sent him a long letter *De Adoratione Divina* and a copy of his *De Vita Libri Tres* (1492). Bindaccio compiled a catalogue of Ficino's works and sent it together with a letter to the physician Gregorio Alessandrino. Both letter and catalogue were published in the first edition of Ficino's *De Sole et Lumine* (1493). Corsi dedicated his *Life of Marsilio Ficino* to Bindaccio.

Passerini, *Genealogia e Storia della Famiglia Ricasoli*, Florence, 1861, p. 155; Della Torre, pp. 59–60, 732–3; *Sup. Fic.*, I, p. 124; Cosenza, p. 604–5.

Bernardo Rucellai (1449–1514): distinguished Florentine statesman and humanist who held many public offices, including that of *Gonfaloniere di Giustizia*. He travelled on diplomatic missions for Lorenzo de'Medici to Milan and later Naples during a crucial period following the wars of the Pazzi conspiracy. After the fall of the Medici he opposed the regime of Piero Soderini, withdrew from politics and went into voluntary exile (1506–10), only returning to Florence a few years before his death. Rucellai presided over the gatherings of a celebrated circle of *literati*—the

Orti Oricellari, named after the Rucellai gardens in which they were held. This circle included Machiavelli and Diacceto. Bernardo's father, Giovanni Rucellai, once consulted Ficino on the relation of *virtu* to *fortuna*, and Bernardo became one of Ficino's closest friends.

His main work is *De Urbe Roma*. He also wrote a history of Florence, *Historiae Florentinae*, which prompted Erasmus to compare its author to Sallust.

Passineri, *Genealogia e Storia della Famiglia Rucellai*, Florence, 1861, p. 122 *seq*; G. Pellegrini, *L'Umanista B. Rucellai e le Sue Opere Storiche*, Livorno, 1920; F. Gilbert, 'Bernardo Rucellai and the Orti Oricellari', in *Journal of the Warburg and Courtauld Institute*, 12, 1949; Della Torre, p. 824; *Sup. Fic.*, I, p. 129.

Sebastiano Salvini of Castel San Niccoli: Ficino's cousin, priest and member of the Florentine College of theologians. He acted as Ficino's secretary. When Ficino was invited in 1482 to go to Hungary by King Matthias to teach Plato's philosophy, he declined the invitation and tried unsuccessfully to induce Salvini to go instead. Salvini's letters are preserved in a Vatican library manuscript (Vat. Lat. 5140).

P. O. Kristeller, 'Sebastiano Salvini, a Florentine humanist and theologian, and a member of Marsilio Ficino's Platonic Academy', in *Didascalie*, ed. Sesto Prete, New York, 1961, pp. 205–43; Della Torre, pp. 94–104; Cosenza, p. 3164–5.

Pope Sixtus IV, (Francesco della Rovere) (1414–1484): eminent Franciscan scholar and theologian, Vicar General of his Order, was made a Cardinal by Pope Paul II. He succeeded to the Pontificate in 1471. He undertook to reform the church and instituted a Jubilee to be celebrated every twenty five years. His nephew Girolamo Riario masterminded the Pazzi conspiracy against the Medici, which the Pope supported. Ficino addressed an open letter to Sixtus IV (*Opera*, p. 808) during the wars following the Pazzi conspiracy to persuade him to make peace with Florence. The Pope was severely criticized on account of his nepotism. Sixtus re-organised the Vatican Library, appointing Platina its Librarian in 1475. He also re-established the Academia Pomponiana, which Paul II had dissolved in 1468. He wrote a number of theological works.

Pastor, *History of the Popes*, IV, p. 17; Della Torre, p. 820; Cosenza, pp. 3286–7.

Giorgio Antonio Vespucci (1435–1514): priest and Canon of Florence Cathedral. He was an early member of Ficino's Academy and became an eminent tutor of the classics. He built up a rich library of Greek and Latin manuscripts. He was one of the six scholars to whom Ficino gave his translations of Plato to revise. Vespucci later entered the monastery of San Marco and became a Dominican under Savonarola. He was an uncle of the famous navigator and explorer, Amerigo Vespucci (after whom America is named). Landino praised Vespucci in his dialogue *De Vera Nobilitate*.

Bandini, *Vita e Lettere di Amerigo Vespucci*, Florence, 1745; Della Torre, pp. 772–4; *Sup. Fic.*, I, pp. 111–2; Cosenza, pp. 3654–5.

Introductory Note to Corsi's 'Life of Marsilio Ficino'

CORSI's *Life of Marsilio Ficino* was written in 1506, some seven years after Ficino's death. Corsi was not one of Ficino's disciples and apparently never knew him personally, but he was acquainted with many of Ficino's former friends and followers, such as the Rucellai and the Ricasoli, from whom he could have acquired the material for this biography. The *Life* is valuable as a near contemporary document, but in places is inaccurate and unreliable as a source of information on Ficino's works and their dating. It does shed some light, however, on the early part of Ficino's life, about which relatively little is known. Some of Corsi's statements are confirmed by Ficino in his own writings, such as, for example, the anecdote concerning Cosimo's choice of Ficino when he was still a boy to be the head of the new Platonic Academy of Florence. But other episodes, such as Ficino's supposed visit to Bologna to study medicine, remain conjectural since no independent evidence has been produced to corroborate Corsi's statements.

Corsi appears to have been only superficially acquainted with Ficino's writings. He relied, to some extent, on the catalogue of the *Works* appended to the 1493 edition of Ficino's *De Sole et Lumine* which, according to Kristeller, would account for some of his errors regarding titles.[1] Corsi's most questionable statement concerns the *Letters*; why he should have cast doubt on their authenticity remains unanswered (see Corsi, XIII, XX). Kristeller puts forward the view that the reasons were political, since some letters are addressed to members of the Valori and Soderini families who belonged to the anti-Medici faction.[2] Marcel claims that Corsi was only questioning the authenticity of the titles and the names of addressees.[3] It is hard to draw any firm conclusion since the two passages in which Corsi refers to the letters are somewhat ambiguous. In only one instance was the name of an addressee intentionally deleted: the name of Bernardo Pulci was deleted in one letter (*Opera*, p. 661.1; *Letters* Vol I. letter 114). The *Letters* were printed in Venice in 1495, some eleven years before Corsi wrote his *Life*, and their authenticity had never been in question. The nephew Corsi refers to (XIII, XX) was Ficino Ficini, who could have assisted in the editing of the *Letters* as he was close to Ficino in the last years of his life.

The translators have been induced to offer this translation of Corsi's *Life of Marsilio Ficino* because of the significant parallels to be drawn between it and Ficino's *Life of Plato*, such as Ficino's close imitation of Plato's way of life and the Platonic Academy itself.

The text which the translators have used is the one printed in Marcel, *Marsile Ficin*, Appendix I, pp. 680–89, a version corrected by the author, and preserved in the Biblioteca Estense, Modena (MS Campori Appendice 310. yt VI. 16). Campori MS variants given by Kristeller in *Studies*, pp. 207–11, have also been consulted.

NOTES

1 See P. O. Kristeller, 'Per La Biografia di Marsilio Ficino' in *Studies in Renaissance Thought and Letters*, p. 194.
2 Ibid, p. 194. See also P. O. Kristeller, 'Un Uomo di Stato e Umanista Fiorentino Giovanni Corsi' in *Studies*, pp. 176–7.
3 Marcel, *Marsile Ficin*, pp. 24–25.

'The Life of Marsilio Ficino' by Giovanni Corsi

Giovanni Corsi to Bindaccio da Ricasoli: greetings.

I REALISED, Bindaccio, that you who normally bear things well, were trying in vain to restrain the grief which you recently suffered at the departure of our Bernardo Rucellai. It is in your nature to be deeply moved by the loss of the most delightful companionship of such a great man on his recent departure for France. I thought that I could remove your sorrow by recalling your spirit from its longing for a most beloved man, leading it to dwell once more on the memory of your Marsilio Ficino, since in this you have frequently been happy to find rest. For when I had decided to make a methodical description of all that is best and most memorable in his life and conduct, you above all seemed to me worthy of this gift, you who will be able not only to wipe away your vexation and bitterness of spirit, but also to render your solitude gentle and pleasing by the memory of that great man. For it very frequently happens that just as noble natures are inspired to glory and virtue by the examples of illustrious men—a fact noted by the ancients concerning Quintus Maximus and Publius Scipio[1]—so by frequently recalling our friends all trace of sickness and sadness of spirit is driven from us. Who indeed was dearer and sweeter to you than Marsilio while he lived? Who was more pleasing and welcome to Marsilio than you? But enough! Accept this work on the man. Farewell.

Florence, 19th April, 1506.

I

WHEN I considered writing about the life and character of Marsilio
Ficino, who as guide penetrated the innermost sanctuary of the
divine Plato, sealed for so many centuries, and thoroughly explored
the whole of his Academy, the first noteworthy thing which came
to mind and encouraged me to write about this man was that he
himself not only investigated its precepts and mysteries but also
penetrated, laid open, and then expounded them to others. This was
something which no one else for the previous thousand years so
much as attempted, let alone accomplished. This was made possible
by the astonishing fecundity of his mind, his burning zeal, and his
extraordinary indifference to all pleasure and, above all, to material
wealth. No less important was the gracious generosity of the princes
under whom he lived, without which these qualities would have
been in vain: in this way that saying came to be more readily
understood: 'Lovers of wisdom cannot achieve much without good
princes, nor again can those princes govern the state without wise
men.'² But I come to the life of Marsilio.

II

Marsilio was a native of Florence, of stock that was neither very
humble nor particularly distinguished. His father, Ficino, was an
eminent doctor especially skilled in surgery, in which he far sur-
passed all others of his time. For this reason many men of the highest
nobility were indebted to him. And above all he was beloved by the
Medici, who then held the first place in the Republic.

III

He was born on the 19th October, 1433, at the time when Cosimo
de' Medici was driven into exile to Venice by a faction of hostile
citizens. Of his early childhood little is known. His first schooling
was under extremely petty and dull tutors a situation which arose
from straitened family circumstances rather than from a lack of
better tutors, for we have gathered that Ficino's father worked
without care for reward. In fact, before the turn of the year, a short

time after the Republic had been established, Cosimo was recalled home.

Cosimo made up his mind to omit nothing which would provide immortality for himself and his country. He was the one man entirely devoted to giving everything its true praise. For this reason he had the highest regard for the study of fine literature, almost extinct at the time, which he did his utmost to revive. Those who showed the mark of genius he favoured with that remarkable generosity of his, raised them up, and advanced them to riches and honours; judging, and rightly so, that all tokens of praise soon perish unless there is a faithful and permanent written record.

IV

Meanwhile the Council of Florence[3] was convened at which, with Pope Eugene presiding, the heresy of the Greeks was thoroughly discussed. With the Greek Emperor came a great many men, highly distinguished in both intellect and learning. Amongst these were Nicholas of Euboea, very learned in both Greek and Latin, and the famous Gemistos Plethon, called by Marsilio a second Plato, and acclaimed equally for his eloquence and his scholarship. When Cosimo heard him frequently discoursing before the scholars and winning their highest applause and admiration, it is said that he was set ablaze with an extraordinary desire to recall to Italy as soon as possible the philosophy of Plato, as of ancient right.

Not many years later, as if by divine fate, he was able to accomplish this through Marsilio,[4] who in his youth had been widely instructed in the humanities and was so kindled with a love of Plato, having been won over to him through Cicero, that, laying all else aside, he pondered this one thing: how, in entering within the portals of the Academy, he might be able to see Plato at closer quarters and speak face to face with him and all his family; that very Plato whom almost all call divine, or even the god of philosophers. Thus, ever-watchful and alert, Ficino gathered extracts from a wide selection of Latin authors; in short, he left nothing undone which he believed would be beneficial to the work undertaken. On this account he always had to hand all the Latin Platonists, namely Cicero, Macrobius, Apuleius, Boethius, St. Augustine, Calcidius, and other like-minded writers, about whom at that time he wrote a great deal which has never been published. Soon afterwards he left these writings in the care of Filippo Valori, a nobleman and one of his foremost pupils.

V

While Marsilio was considering these things, he was at last driven quite unwillingly to Bologna, by his father's insistence and by dire financial straits. Here, having left the Academy[5] behind, he studied the Aristotelians and even the modern writers, from whom he had for a long time shrunk both by nature and inclination, in order that he too might soon practise his father's art of medicine. But clearly by divine grace, on one occasion when he visited Florence and was taken by his father to pay his respects to Cosimo, it is said that Cosimo, perceiving the genius of the young man and recognizing in him the extraordinary desire for study which set him afire, rejoiced greatly as if he had now fully understood that, beyond any doubt, this would be the man whom he had long since chosen to shed light on the philosophy of Plato. And presently summoning Ficino, he exhorted him to take especial care over Marsilio's studies so that he should not go against his natural disposition. He said that there was no reason to take account of domestic hardship, for he would never neglect him in any matter but would supply everything most generously. 'You, Ficino,' he said, 'have been sent to us to heal bodies, but your Marsilio here has been sent down from heaven to heal souls.'[6]

VI

Having this advice from such a great man, Marsilio was filled with hope and turned his mind and spirit wholly to the study of Plato, being now in his twenty-sixth year. Thus in a short time, when he was thoroughly versed in Greek literature, having had Platina[7] as his tutor, so I have heard, he expounded the hymns of Orpheus, and it is said that he sang them to the lyre in the ancient style with remarkable sweetness.

A little later, at Cosimo's instigation, he translated into Latin the book of Hermes Trismegistus *On Divine Wisdom and the Creation of the World*[8]. For this purpose he was endowed by Cosimo with the most generous gift of a family estate at Careggi near the outskirts of the town, as well as with a house in town, and even with beautifully written Greek books of Plato and Plotinus which were very costly, especially in those times.

VII

Not long afterwards, prompted by Cosimo's encouragement and authority, he turned his attention to translating the whole of Plato into Latin, which he completed in the next five years.[9] By this time he was thirty-five years old. Cosimo had already died, but his son Piero succeeded to his estate and to the charge of governing the Republic.[10] Piero was a man of the gentlest disposition, who for humanity and forebearance, not to mention his other virtues, may be compared with any of the greatest princes. At those times when he was seized with gout, he governed the Republic through the aristocratic party. Owing to his health he was allowed to govern for no more than five years, being the period by which he survived his father Cosimo.

Whenever Marsilio visited him, which was frequently, and unfolded the teachings of Platonic philosophy, they had a marvellous effect on Piero. He urged Marsilio to publish his translations of Plato and to interpret and expound them in public, so that his citizens might also be enlightened by the new-found splendour of such sublime doctrine and such fine philosophy. And he personally supplied Marsilio with many volumes of great value, in both Greek and Latin, which greatly helped in setting out and explaining the teachings of Plato. And so at that time Marsilio gave public lectures on Plato's *Philebus* to a large audience.[11] Some lectures of this period are still extant, as well as four volumes of Platonic commentaries.

VIII

Marsilio intended at this time to develop fully the book of *Platonic Theology* almost as a model of the pagan religion, and also to publish the *Orphic Hymns* and *Sacrifices*;[12] but a divine miracle directly hindered him more and more every day, so that he daily accomplished less, being distracted, as he said, by a certain bitterness of spirit. St. Jerome has recorded that the same befell him over the writings of

Cicero.[13] Indeed, it was to lighten his anguish of spirit, if at all possible, that at that time Ficino wrote the *Commentary on Love*.[14] He was persuaded to write this book by Giovanni Cavalcanti, a nobleman especially dear to Marsilio, with the aim of countering his anguish and at the same time calling the lovers of empty beauty back to immortal beauty. He attempted, moreover, to refresh his mind in many other ways, but all to no purpose. At length he came fully to realize that he was suffering these things through some divine influence because he had strayed too far from the Christian thinkers.[15] For this reason, with a change of heart, he interpreted the *Platonic Theology*[16] itself according to the Christian tradition, producing eighteen books on this subject. Besides this, he wrote his book *On the Christian Religion*[17] and undoubtedly obtained peace and consolation through these studies, completely dispelling all that bitterness of spirit.[18] But now, whilst he was still in his forty-second year from being a pagan he became a soldier of Christ.[19] He left the whole of his patrimony to his brothers, for he received an adequate living from the two parishes whose care he had assumed through Lorenzo de' Medici.

IX

This was that great Lorenzo, son of Piero and grandson of Cosimo, both of whom we have mentioned before. To the Florentine Republic he was Augustus, to the liberal arts Maecenas. For while he was alive there was no branch of learning, however obscure, which did not flower or was not given its due; and at that time the city of Florence was universally called a second Athens on account of the gathering of such learned men. Hence, with good reason, one of the learned men has written thus: 'Indeed the studies of letters owed most to the Florentines; amongst the Florentines, most to the Medici; amongst the Medici, most to Lorenzo.'[20] It is therefore the calamity of our times, and utterly deplorable, that in our State, in place of instruction and the liberal arts, ignorance and lack of knowledge prevail; in place of modesty and restraint, ambition and excess; in place of generosity, greed. And so much so that nothing at all is done for the Republic, nothing for the laws, but all things are done for pleasure; thus it is that all the best men are assailed by the people as objects of derision. Bernardo Rucellai, detesting the Republic as a most barbaric stepmother, considered he would rather go into exile than remain any longer in that city, from which the disciplines of all the liberal arts and the best institutions of our ancestors, together with the Medici, were banished.

X

But I return to Marsilio who, besides those things which he had written so far, produced a book entitled *Remedy for the Plague*,[21] and another on the beliefs of all philosophers (that is, what their opinions were on God and the soul)[22] and then *Three Books On Life*.[23] He then devoted himself entirely to those summaries of all Plato's works,[24] which he had long wanted to produce. In a short time he published these, divided into fixty-six parts for everyone to read, and with these also the *Platonic Theology* about which we spoke a little earlier, which he then expounded at his home over a period of nearly three years to most of his friends, and also afterwards in public, with Pico della Mirandola and the foremost of the nobility in the audience. At the same time he wrote *On Pleasure*[25] as well.

XI

Being then fifty-one years old, he undertook the translation of Plotinus, in response to the entreaties of Pico della Mirandola. He had just begun this when, through the agency of Lorenzo de' Medici, he was received into the Florentine Chapter of Canons.[26] This was no small honour and gave very great joy to his colleagues and to all the citizens. At that time he expounded the divine gospels[27] in public before a crowded assembly to the great gratitude of all. In the next five years he presented the whole of Plotinus in Latin, and produced annotated commentaries[28] on each of the fifty four books. For such excellent work he earned universal acclaim, since this is that Plotinus whom Platonists themselves scarcely understand even after much toil, so concise his language, so deep his teaching! Consequently Marsilio is justly praised, for he was the first of all the Latin writers to uncover and elucidate the most obscure enigmas (I will not say doctrines) of such a great philosopher.

XII

After these works he translated Synesius *On Dreams*,[29] Psellus *On Daemons*, Iamblichus *On the Mysteries of the Egyptians*, Priscian of Lydia *On Theophrastus Concerning the Soul* (with additions by the same Priscian), on which he also wrote commentaries. At the same time he translated Porphyry's *On Fasting* and *Means for Reaching the Divine*, also much from Hermias *On the Phaedrus*, from Iamblichus *On the Pythagorean School* and from Theon of Smyrna *On Mathematics*. He also translated Alcinous's *Summary of Plato*, together with the *Definitions* of Speusippus, the *Sayings* of Pythagoras, and Xenocrates' *On Consolation*, as well as the extracts from Athenagoras' *On Resurrection*. Furthermore he translated from Greek into Latin several works of Proclus, namely, *On Alcibiades, On The Republic*, and *On Priesthood*. He was then in his fifty-eighth year.

XIII

Having published Plotinus, he devoted himself completely to translating the books of Dionysius the Areopagite[30] into Latin, since they especially supported the Christian religion and in no way departed from the Platonic discipline. In addition, twelve volumes of the letters of Marsilio to many of his friends were circulated, with fabricated headings,[31] wrongly addressed, except for a very few letters concerning speculative philosophy, scattered throughout the volumes, namely: *On the Five Keys to Platonic Theology*[32] and in the same group: *On the Rapture of Paul into the Third Heaven*,[33] *On Light*,[34] *On the Star of the Magi*,[35] and some others of this kind, written with the greatest learning and skill. All the others should be ascribed to Ficino,[36] his brother's son.

XIV

In the last seven years of his life, after he had published what he had written on *Plato's Fatal Number*[37] from the eighth book of *The Republic*, and then *On the Sun and Light*,[38] he began new commentaries on the whole of Plato and then a most useful division of Plato's work into separate books,[39] so that the mind of the writer might be more easily and clearly understood. In that year, when he had finished highly learned commentaries on *Parmenides*[40] and *Timaeus*,[41] he also wrote and completed commentaries on *The Mystical Theology* of Dionysius and then on *Divine Names*.[42] Indeed in this last period he published commentaries not only on *Parmenides*, *Timaeus* and on *Theaetetus* but also on *Philebus*, *Phaedrus* and *The Sophist*.[43] And at this time, in addition he publicly expounded to a great gathering the epistles of St. Paul.[44] He began commentaries on these, but he was overtaken by death and left them unfinished.

XV

So much for Marsilio's writings, as they are at present known to us. It remains to recount something of the life and character of the man.

In stature he was very short, of slender build, and somewhat hunched in both shoulders. He was a little hesitant of speech and stuttered, but only in pronouncing the letter 's'; yet in his speech and appearance he was not without grace. His legs and arms, and particularly his hands, were rather long. His face was drawn forward and presented a mild and pleasing aspect; his complexion was ruddy. His hair was golden and curly and stood up above his forehead. His bodily constitution contained excessive blood which was mixed with a thin subtle red bile. His health was not at all settled, for he suffered very much from a weakness of the stomach, and although he always appeared cheerful and festive in company, yet it was thought that he sat long in solitude and became as if numb with melancholy. This came about either from black bile produced by the excessive burning of bile through continual night study,[45] or, as he himself said, from Saturn, which at his birth was in the ascendant in Aquarius and nearly square to Mars in Scorpio.[46]

XVI

After his forty-fifth year he enjoyed somewhat better health, although during the whole of his life, as I have said, he was never fully healthy. Though he was often sick, and gravely so, and there were fears for his life, his health was restored through the prayers of many friends on his behalf and he reached his sixty-sixth year. By nature he was mild, refined and gentle, although sometimes he was quick to break out into anger when driven by bile, yet like a flash of lightning he instantly became calm again. He easily forgot injury, but was never forgetful of obligations. He was not at all inclined to excessive desire; yet he was enraptured by love just as Socrates was, and he used to discuss and debate the subject of love in the Socratic manner with young men. When he was engaged with them in this way, the more he cherished them, the more they honoured and respected him. Throughout his life he was content with simple clothes and possessions. He was neat rather than elegant and was strongly averse to all extravagance. He obtained the necessities of life readily enough; otherwise he was sparing in food,. but he did select the most excellent wines. For he was rather disposed towards wine, yet he never went away from parties drunk or fuddled, though often more cheerful.

XVII

There were frequent but well-ordered feasts at his own or his friends' houses, and especially at those of the Medici,[47] by whom he was often invited. As I have said, he was as mild and gentle in discussion as in everything else, ever cheerful and an excellent conversationalist, second to none in refinement and wit. Many of his sayings survive, as they were uttered, in the Tuscan language. Every day these sayings, full of wit, jests and laughter, are commonly on the lips of his friends. Even now, from time to time, the cunning man, as the poet says, may play with these upon the heart.[48] But to repeat them individually, besides taking too long, would sound out of place: a consequence of the limitations of the language, the novelty of the subject and the particular qualities of his native tongue.

XVIII

In inventiveness he was always fluent and resourceful; in debate he was not so effective or ready: thus he remained essentially a poet. His style was appropriate and becoming to philosophy. He was always content with his lot, so that at no time was he moved by the desire to squander or accumulate. Indeed, as befits a philosopher, he was rather indifferent to business matters.

He attended carefully not only to his own health but to that of all his friends as well, for he shared the fruits of his not inconsiderable study of medicine, effecting remarkable cures always free of charge.

XIX

It was wonderful to see the healing skill with which he cured some afflicted by black bile, restoring them to perfect health. The Medici would summon him first whenever the need arose and he worked for this family with untiring dedication to restore the health of many of its members. He also paid attention to many aspects of physiognomy,[49] in which, through considerable study undertaken in early manhood, he had become an excellent practitioner. Astronomy, too, he studied with unusual care and earned much praise in this subject, particularly in his refutations of the astrologers.[50] He shunned as being worse than dogs and serpents[51] all casters of horoscopes, charlatans and disputatious scholastics, Aristotelians, and those addicted to the modern school.

XX

Here is something not to be left out: he had a unique and divine skill in magic, driving out evil demons and spirits from very many places and putting them to flight. Always a very keen defender of religion, he was extremely hostile to superstition. Although very eager to encourage the fine arts, he always had an especial inclination towards the Platonic teachings. He would take great pains to reconcile friends. He was a model of dutiful conduct towards parents, relatives, friends and the dead, but particularly towards his mother, Alessandra,[52] whose life he prolonged, by remarkable care and attention, to her eighty-fourth year, even though she was an invalid. He lived frequently in the countryside near the city.

On serious matters he always responded instantly to the entreaties of his friends, helping them if necessary with the strong authority and influence which he wielded with all the Medici. He was swift to comfort those afflicted by misfortune; indeed, he exercised more gentleness in comforting those in distress than severity in reproving wrongdoers. In short, he showed humanity, gentleness, and love to all alike.

It is easy to appreciate how many friends he had and the kind of people they were from the dedications of his books, and also from the volumes of letters which, as I have stated earlier, were mostly brought together and put in order by Ficino's nephew. But among others who kept him intimate company almost daily were Bernardo Rucellai, Giovanni Canacci and Bindaccio Ricasoli. These were men of unimpeachable integrity and learning; in the words of the poet, 'the Earth has borne none more fair.'[53]

Bernardo was outstanding for his lofty spirit and his authority so that in the conduct of affairs his skill was second to none of his age. He was preeminent as a man of letters, and pure in speech. His was a free spirit, a slave to none. His respect for antiquity was remarkable. In short, there was nothing in the man that did not befit a patrician and a senator; but more of him elsewhere.

Canacci was serious in his ways, grave of speech, agreeably refined and very quick-witted; his character and way of life call to mind the Cincinnati and the ancient Serrani.[54]

Bindaccio had a calm and mild disposition, a very gentle manner and a most generous heart.

With these men Marsilio often used to discuss serious matters of philosophy, and sometimes he would jest and converse with them.

XXI

In the last five years of his life he took great delight in the friendship of Bishop Cosimo Pazzi of Arezzo, a man of great virtue, who was outstanding in academic learning and many other skills, 'for far from his home he contended with fortune for a long time, observing the ways of many men; and enduring much on the outward journey but even more on the return.'[55]

Many people advanced to the summit of philosophy under Marsilio, but first among them all were Giovanni Pico della Mirandola, and Francesco da Diacceto, who came from a noble Florentine family. They were two glorious lights of the Academy, two models of virtue. They were an exceptional pair on this earth, but different in character. In Pico could be seen illustrious fortune, remarkable ingenuity, powers which were almost divine, and a wide variety of learning. But in Diacceto fortune was less abundant and nature less versatile. Yet so profound was this man's intellect, so vigorous and absorbed in the study of wisdom, that he was the only person in our time, it seems, to be admitted to the secret mysteries of the Academy. And when Pico openly disagreed with Marsilio, Diacceto always defended and praised his master. But far be it from me to pass judgement on such great men.

I hope that some of Diacceto's commentaries on Plato[56] will soon be published in the common tongue, for they will show to all what a great man he is in every branch of philosophy.

XXII

While he was still alive the fame of Marsilio spread throughout almost the whole world. Thus it was that Pope Sixtus IV,[57] a man of magnanimity and great learning, and many fathers of the distinguished Roman Curia strove with lavish promises to persuade Marsilio to come to Rome. Furthermore, Matthias, King of Hungary, a man of the highest spirit and renown, vied with other princes in offering large rewards for Marsilio to leave Florence and come to spread Plato's teachings.[58] But he was always content with his present circumstances and was not to be enticed by any reasons, prayers or gifts to accept any other situation, however fine and rewarding, at the cost of abandoning the Medici, to whom he owed all that he had been given, together with those friends who were most dear to him, his mother who was now in her old age, and the Academy which was flourishing so well.

XXIII

So he was content with a quiet life, and could not be separated from his native city. Every day men of outstanding intellect and learning used to come from many different places to see and hear him. Pico della Mirandola, that miracle of nature of whom I have spoken above, was one of these. When he came to Florence, he took quite modest rooms near Marsilio and occupied them for almost three years. Furthermore, he sought the gift of Florentine citizenship. There was also Pier Leone,[59] who was easily the leading physician of his time as well as a passionate investigator of nature's secrets; he devoted himself assiduously to the Platonists and to Marsilio, whom he always held in the highest honour.

XXIV

This is almost all that I have learned about Marsilio until now. He died on 1st October, 1499, on the very day that Paolo Vitelli,[60] commanding the Florentine army, was enticed out of the Pisan camp and into the city, where he was opposed by a large number of the nobility and lost his life.

Whether death came to Marsilio from old age or, as some maintain, from his stomach ailment, I have not been able to discover. All his friends attended the funeral as well as many of the nobility. Marcello Virgilio[61] made the funeral speech away from the general gathering. Marsilio was buried in the Church of the Santa Reparata in the sepulchre reserved for canons. The people of Florence attended, with grief and tears.

Notes on Corsi's 'Life of Marsilio Ficino'

ABBREVIATIONS

The same abbreviations for references are used here as for the Notes on the Letters: see p. 81.

1 Quintus Fabius Maximus and Publius Scipio were Romans who distinguished themselves by their heroic conduct during the wars against Carthage. See Sallust, *Jugurtha*, Proem, IV, 5–6.

2 Plato, *Republic*, V, 473D.

3 The chief object of the Council of Florence (1438–45) was reunion with the Greek Church, under threat from the Turks. It commenced in Ferrara, but Cosimo de' Medici was instrumental in having it moved to Florence. The main obstacle was the 'Filioque' clause in the Creed of Nicea, which refers to the Holy Spirit as 'proceeding from the Father *and the Son*'. The Greeks held this addition unlawful, while allowing that it was doctrinally unexceptionable. After much argument a measure of union was achieved, but it was always unstable, and ceased altogether after the fall of Constantinople in 1453. The Council did, however, establish that Unity of Faith with Diversity of Rite was the basic principle on which the unity of the Christian Church should be pursued. The Council also provided a unique opportunity for Italian humanists and scholars to meet their Greek counterparts, many of whom now settled in Italy and contributed greatly to the revival of learning.

4 Cosimo's choice of Ficino when he was still a boy (*adhuc puer*) to be the head of the new Platonic Academy is described in the proem to Ficino's epitomes of Plotinus, *Opera*, II, p. 1537.

5 Ficino's Academy had not yet been established. The reference is to the academic or Platonic philosophers.

6 See letter of dedication to Ficino's *De Vita Libri Tres*, *Opera*, p. 493: 'I had two fathers, Ficino the physician and Cosimo de'Medici. I was born from the first and reborn from the second. The first pledged me to Galen, the physician and Platonist, the second dedicated me to the divine Plato; whilst Galen is the physician of the body, Plato is the physician of souls.' *Cf.* Diog. Laert., III, 45

(Life of Plato): 'Phoebus gave to mortals Asclepius and Plato, the one to save their bodies, the other to save their souls.'

7 Platina is mentioned in Ficino's list of friends (*Catalogus familiarium*) *Opera*, p. 937. Platina spent a period of time in Florence from 1457 to 1462, but nothing is known about his supposed friendship with Ficino.

8 *Opera*, p. 1836. This translation was made in 1463.

9 Ficino worked on these translations from 1463 to 1468 but continued to revise them after this date, right up to 1484, when the first printed edition appeared.

10 Cosimo de'Medici died in August, 1464. Ficino dedicated his translation of Xenocrates' *De Morte* to Piero de'Medici, addressing him as 'Pillar of the Academy': see Ficino, *Opera*, p. 1965.

11 According to Kristeller, *Studies*, p. 111, and Marcel, p. 309, the Church in Florence where these lectures were held, could have been the old Santa Maria degli Angeli. See also Michael Allen, *Marsilio Ficino: The Philebus Commentary*, p. 8, and footnote 31.

12 An anonymous Latin version of the Orphic hymns is found in two manuscripts, Laur. 36, 35 and Ottob. Lat. 2966. The *Sacrifices* refers possibly to Proclus, *De Sacrificio et Magia*. See *Opera*, p. 1928, and Marcel, p. 347.

13 See Jerome, *Epistles XXII*, 30 (to Eustochius). Jerome fell ill with a fever and in a vision was admonished for being a follower of Cicero rather than of Christ. On awaking from the dream, his conscience so tormented him that henceforth he read the books of God with more devotion than he had previously given to the books of men.

14 *De Amore*, a commentary on Plato's *Symposium* (*Opera*, p. 1320) written about 1469.

15 Ficino, in a letter to Francesco Marescalchi written in 1474 (*Opera*, p. 644.3) speaks of not yet having finished writing the book *On The Christian Religion* because of a severe illness from which he despaired of recovering. Prayer brought immediate relief and Ficino concluded that this was a sign from God that in future he should declare the Christian teaching with greater zeal. See *Letters*, Vol. 1, p. 126.

16 *Theologia Platonica sive de Immortalitate Animarum*, *Opera* I, p. 78, *et seq.*, written between 1469 and 1474.

17 *De Christiana Religione*, *Opera*, p. 1 *et seq.*, written *c.* 1474.

18 Ficino suffered from attacks of melancholy at different times during his life. On one occasion (in 1476) Cavalcanti wrote to him, lightheartedly accusing him of attaching excessive importance to the influence upon him of the stars, especially Saturn. See *Letters*, Vol. 2, p. 31. See also note 46 below.

19 In fact, Ficino was ordained a priest in 1473 (at the age of 40). See a letter addressed to Lorenzo de'Medici in which Ficino thanks him for bestowing on him the parish church of San Cristoforo in Novoli, near Florence. See *Letters*, Vol. 1, p. 63.

20 Poliziano, *Epistolae*, XII, 32.

21 *Consiglio Contra la Pestilentia*, written in Italian during the Plague of 1478–9. It was translated into Latin by Girolamo Ricci in 1516 and included in the Basle edition of Ficino's works (*Opera*, p. 576).

22 *Di Dio et Anima*, addressed to Francesco Capponi (1457); see *Sup. Fic.*, II, p. 128 *et seq.*

23 *De Vita Libri Tres, Opera*, p. 493. Completed in 1489.

24 The epitomes or summaries contain the main arguments of each dialogue. Kristeller believes Ficino wrote the *argumentum* to each dialogue at the same time as he translated it. See *Sup. Fic.*, I, pp. xi, cxvi.

25 *De Voluptate*, addressed to Antonio Canigiani; in fact written much earlier, in 1457; *Opera*, p. 986.

26 He was made a canon in 1487, at the age of 54.

27 A collection of sermons (*Praedicationes*) are printed in *Opera*, p. 473. See also *Sup. Fic.*, I, lxxxii.

28 The summaries are printed in *Opera*, p. 1538 *et seq.* The translation and commentary were completed in 1490 and published in 1492.

29 The works referred to in this Section are as follows:
   Synesii de Somniis (*Opera*, p. 1968), *c.* 1488. See *Sup. Fic.* I, cxxxvii.
   Pselli de Demonibus (*Opera*, p. 1939), *c.* 1488, excerpts.
   Iamblichi de Mysteriis (*Opera*, p. 1873), 1488.
   Prisciani Lydii super Theophrastum (*Opera*, p. 1801) *et seq.*
   Porphyrii de Abstinentia (*Opera*, p. 1932) excerpts.
   Porphyrii de Occasionibus (*Opera*, p. 1929), *c.* 1488.
   Hermiae Commentarium in Phaedrum Platonis (MS Vat. Lat. 5953);
      not included in *Opera*; see *Sup. Fic.* I, cxlvi.
   Iamblichi de Secta Pythagorica Libri IV (MS Vat. Lat. 5953),
      written before 1474.
   Theonis Smyrnei de Locis Mathematicis (MS Vat. Lat. 4530);
      see *Sup. Fic.* I, cxlvi.
   Alcinoi de Doctrina Platonis (*Opera*, p. 1945), 1464.
   Speusippi Definitiones (*Opera*, p. 1962), written before 1464.
   Pythagorae Aurea Verba (*Opera*, p. 1978), written before 1464.
   Xenocratis de Morte (*Opera*, p. 1965), *c.* 1464.
   Athenagorae de Resurrectione (*Opera*, p. 1871), excerpts written before 1493.
   Ex Proculi Commentariis in Alcibiadem Platonis Primum (*Opera*, p. 1908),
      1488, excerpts.
   Procli de Sacrificio et Magia (*Opera*, p. 1928), 1488.

30 *De Mystica Theologia, De Divinis Nominibus* (*Opera*, p. 1013), translation and commentary 1492, dedicated to Cardinal Giovanni de' Medici.

31 See Introductory Note to Corsi's *Life of Marsilio Ficino*, p. 133.

32 *Quinque Platonicae Sapientiae Claves, Opera*, p. 682, *et seq.* (an earlier redaction of some of the shorter treatises later included in the second book of *Letters*) 1476. For a corrected text see Marcel, *Theologie Platonicienne*, Vol. III, *Opuscula Theologica*, pp. 301–43.

33 *De Raptu Pauli* (*Opera*, p. 697), 1476.

34 *De Lumine*, which forms part of the second book of *Letters* (*Opera*, p. 717) written in 1476; a later enlarged version written in 1492 is also printed in the *Opera*, p. 976 *et seq.*

35 *Divina lex fieri a coelo non potest, Opera*, p. 849 (from the seventh book of *Letters*); 'Divine law cannot arise from the stars'. *De Stella Magorum, Opera*, p. 489.

36 This was Ficino Ficini, who was executed in 1530 for his Medici sympathies. He was a disciple of Diacceto. See *Sup. Fic.*, II, p. 334.

37 *Commentarius in Loco Platonis ex Octavo Libro de Republica de Mutatione Reipublicae per Numerum Fatalem (Opera*, p. 1413), written *c.* 1496. See *Republic*, VIII, 546–7. This section deals with the manner in which the ideal state ruled by the guardians begins to decline through lack of knowledge concerning the law of number relating to human birth.

38 *De Sole et Lumine (Opera*, p. 965), 1493.

39 Ficino did not start new commentaries on the whole of Plato at this time. Between 1490 and 1496 he completed his revisions of the commentaries, putting them together and dividing them into separate chapter headings and summaries of contents. The only new commentaries written at this period were the *Parmenides* and *Sophist* commentaries (1494) and a commentary on a section of book VIII of the *Republic* (1496) (See note 37 above). The final collected commentaries on Plato were published in 1496.

40 *Commentarius in Parmenidem (Opera*, p. 1136 *seq.*) written *c.* 1494.

41 *In Timaeum Commentarius (Opera*, p. 1438 *seq.*). This contains the second version, written about 1484. An earlier version, written possibly before 1452, is not extant. According to Kristeller the earlier version may be identical with the lost work entitled *Principles of Platonic Discipline*, mentioned by Ficino in two letters (*Opera*, p. 619.3 and p. 929.2). See *Sup. Fic.*, I, cxx, clxiii.

42 See note 30, above.

43 *Commentarii in Philebum (Opera*, p. 1207) *Commentarius in Phaedrum (Opera*, p. 1363) *Commentarius in Sophistam (Opera*, p. 1285). There is no commentary on *Theaetetus*.

44 *In Epistolas Divi Pauli (Opera*, p. 425).

45 Black bile (μελαινα χολη) was one of the four bodily humours recognised by medieval physicians. It is associated with the element earth and the qualities cold and dry. It gives rise to men of melancholy temperament who are influenced by the planet Saturn. When of pure quality and present in correct quantity it is responsible for the fine work of men of outstanding intellect and wisdom. When impure, in excess, or produced by burning of any of the humours it causes excitement and frenzy, followed by dullness, foolishness, depression and madness.

   Ficino, himself subject to melancholy, describes these states and their prevention and cure in *De Vita Libri Tres* I, 3–7 and 10–18. See also Hippocrates, *The Nature of Man;* Galen, *On the Natural Faculties*, II, ix.

46 In a letter to Cavalcanti (*Opera*, p. 733.1) Ficino discusses his horoscope: 'Saturn seems to have impressed the seal of melancholy on me from the beginning, set as it is, almost in the midst of my ascendant Aquarius. It is influenced by Mars . . . it is in square aspect to the Sun and Mercury in Scorpio.' See *Letters*, Vol. 2, letter 24. See also note 18 above.

47 One feast of this kind, described in *De Amore* and in a letter to Jacopo Bracciolini, was celebrated by Lorenzo de' Medici in his villa at Careggi in honour of Plato's

birthday on the 7th November 1468. Another feast was held by Francesco Bandini at his house in Florence, probably in November 1473. See *Letters*, Vol. 1, letter 107. The nature of the Platonic convivium is described by Ficino in a letter to Bembo. See *Letters*, Vol. 2, letter 42.

48 Persius, *Satires*, I, 116–7.

49 A lost work on physiognomy is mentioned by Ficino in one letter (*Opera*, p. 619.3). See *Sup. Fic.*, I, clxiii.

50 See Ficino's *Disputatio Contra Iudicium Astrologorum, Sup. Fic.* II p. 11 *et seq.*; also letter 37 in this volume.

51 'Cane pejus et angue', Horace, *Epistles*, I, XVII, 30.

52 Alessandra di Nannocio Diotifeci, who died about 1498, one year before Ficino.

53 Horace, *Satires*, I, V, 41.

54 Cincinnatus was the surname of L. Quintius, who was summoned by the Senate from his modest farm to assume the office of *Dictator* when Rome was threatened by hostile forces. He returned to his farm when the danger had passed. Serranus was the surname of Attilius Regulus who was also summoned from his farm to public office during a period of crisis.

55 Homer, *Odyssey*, I, 1–5.

56 Corsi may be referring to Diacceto's treatise on love, *De Amore*. An Italian version of this work was also prepared by Diacceto. The *Panegyricus in Amorem*, which is dedicated to Corsi, was also translated into Italian.

57 There is no evidence that Pope Sixtus IV ever invited Ficino to Rome, but see a letter to Ficino from Ermolao Barbaro (*Opera*, p. 912.3), stating that the Pope (Innocent VIII) had spoken very highly of Ficino and wished to see him in Rome.

58 See letter 39 in this volume. See also a letter to Nicolaus Bathory, written in 1482 (*Opera*, p. 884.2), in which Ficino declined an invitation from King Matthias to go to Hungary to teach Plato's philosophy.

59 See Notes on Ficino's Correspondents under Pier Leone.

60 Paolo Vitelli and his brother Vitelozzo were suspected by the anti-Medici faction, who were then in control of Florence, of being in league with the Medici. Paolo was led into a trap and hung by a hostile crowd.

61 See Notes on Ficino's Correspondents under Marcello Virgilio Adriani.

Bibliography

In addition to the publications listed below, the reader is also referred to the bibliography in *The Letters of Marsilio Ficino, Vol. 1*, p. 235 *seq.*, and to that in *The Philosophy of Marsilio Ficino* by P. O. Kristeller, German ed. 1972, p. 387 *seq.*

TEXT OF WORKS BY FICINO

Ficinus, M.: *Opera Omnia*, 2 vols., Basle, 1561; 2nd ed., 1576; Paris, 1641. 1576 ed. reprint in 1959, Bottega d'Erasmo, Turin.
—— *Epistolae Libri XII*, Venice, 1495; Nuremberg, 1497;? Prague, 1500.
Kristeller, P. O. (ed.): *Supplementum Ficinianum—Marsilii Ficini Florentini opuscula inedita et dispersa*, Florence, 1937. Reprint in 1973.
Kristeller, P. O.: *Studies in Renaissance Thought and Letters*, Rome, 1956, 1969; containing unpublished writings of Ficino, with additional notes on the manuscripts and printed editions of his works not included in the *Supplementum*.

TRANSLATIONS

Allen, M.: *Marsilio Ficino: The Philebus Commentary*, University of California, Los Angeles, 1975. Text and translation of Ficino's *Commentarium in Philebum Platonis de Summo Bono*.
Boer, C.: *Marsilio Ficino: The Book of Life*, University of Dallas, Texas, 1980. An English translation of Ficino's *De Vita Libri Tres*.
Figliucci, F.: *Le Divine Lettere del Gran Marsilio Ficino*, Venice, 1546, 1563. An Italian translation of the twelve books of letters.
Jayne, S. R.: 'Marsilio Ficino's Commentary on Plato's Symposium', *University of Missouri Studies* XIX, no. 1, Columbia, 1944. Text and translation of Ficino's *De Amore*.
Marcel, R.: *Commentaire sur le Banquet de Platon*, Paris, 1955. Text and French translation of Ficino's *De Amore*.
—— *Théologie Platonicienne de l'Immortalité des Ames*, 3 vols., Paris, 1964–70. Text and French translation of Ficino's *Theologia Platonica Sive de Immortalitate*

Animorum, the third volume containing the text of *Opuscula Theologica* from the second book of letters.

SELECTED STUDIES ON FICINO AND SOURCE MATERIAL

Chastel, A.: *Marsile Ficin et l'Art*, Geneva, 1954. Reprint, 1976.
—— 'Marsile Ficin. Lettres sur la Connaissance de Soi et sur l'Astrologie' in *La Table Ronde*, 2(1945), a French translation of selected letters, including letters 10, 22, 23 and 24 of Volume 2.
—— 'L'Apocalypse en 1500: La Fresque de l'Antéchrist à la Chapelle Saint-Brice d'Orvieto, in *Bibliothèque d'Humanisme et Renaissance*, XIV (1952), pp. 124–40, a French translation of Ficino's *Apologia Contra Savonarolam*.
Dellá Torre, A.: *Storia dell'Accademia Platonica di Firenze*, Florence, 1902. Reprint 1969, Bottega d'Erasmo, Turin.
Ficino, Marsilio: *Lessico Greco-Latino*, ed. R. Pintaudi, Rome, 1977 (Ateneo e Bizzarri).
Garin, E.: *La Cultura Filosofica del Rinascimento Italiano*, Florence, 1979.
—— *Prosatori Latini del Quattrocento*, Milan, 1952. Contains an Italian translation of Ficino's *De Sole*.
The Hymns of Orpheus, tr. T. Taylor, in *Thomas Taylor, Selected Writings*, ed. Kathleen Raine, G. M. Harper, London, 1969.
Iamblichus: *Life of Pythagoras*, tr. T. Taylor, London, 1818.
Kristeller, P. O.: *The Philosophy of Marsilio Ficino*, Columbia University, 1943. Reprint 1964; Italian ed., Florence, 1953; German ed., Frankfurt, 1972.
—— *Renaissance Thought and its Sources*, Columbia Univ. Press, New York, 1979.
—— 'Sebastiano Salvini, a Florentine Humanist and Theologian, and a Member of Marsilio Ficino's Platonic Academy' in *Didascalie*, ed. Sesto Prete, New York, 1961, pp. 205–43.
—— 'Some Original Letters and Autograph Manuscripts of Marsilio Ficino' in *Studi di bibliografia e di Storia in Onore di Tammaro de Marinis*, vol. III, Verona, 1964, pp. 5–33.
Marcel, R.: *Marsile Ficin*, Paris, 1958.
Novotny, F.: *The Posthumous Life of Plato*, Prague, 1977, ch. 20, 'Marsilio Ficino. The Florentine Academy'.
Plato: *The Dialogues of Plato*, tr. Benjamin Jowett (3rd ed.).
—— *The Epistles*, tr. G. R. Morrow, Library of Liberal Arts, 1962.
Porphyry: 'Life of Pythagoras', tr. M. Hadas and M. Smith, in *Heroes and Gods*, London, 1965.
Reumont, A. von.: *Lorenzo de' Medici*, Leipzig, 1883, and London, 1876.
Rochon, A.: *La Jeunesse de Laurent de Medicis (1449–1478)*, Paris, 1963.
Roscoe, W.: *Life of Lorenzo de' Medici*, London, 1884.
St. Augustine of Hippo: *City of God*, tr. H. Bettenson, 1972.
Saitta, G.: *La Filosofia di Marsilio Ficino*, Messina, 1923, 3rd ed., Bologna, 1954.
Schiavone, M.: *Problemi Filosofici in Marsilio Ficino*, Milan, 1957.
Shumaker, Wayne: *The Occult Sciences in the Renaissance*, California, 1972.

Thorndike, L.: *A History of Magic and Experimental Science*, 6 vols., New York, 1923–41.

Trinkaus, C.: *In Our Image and Likeness. Humanity and Divinity in Italian Humanist Thought*, 2 vols., London, 1970.

Zanier, G.: *La Medicina Astrologica e la sua Teoria*, Rome, 1977 (Ateneo e Bizzarri).

Index

Marſiliuſ ficinuſ Bartolomeo ſcale oratori.
legi queſtioneſ chriſtophori Landini camal-
dulenſeſ. In iiſ libriſ maroniſ adyta pene-
trat. Ciceroniſ dialogoſ imitatur ad un-
guem. felicem uirum fabricat feliciſſime.
Lege illoſ & tu. Scio mecum ſentieſ.
Vale. S3 quare T laudando chriſtopho-
ro tam breuiſ eſ marſili? Quia habet neſcio qd quod exprimere nequeaſ.
Iterum uale.

Marſiliuſ ficinuſ laurentio medici Viro
magnanimo. pax tibi. Si paci, docto
& bono ſacerdoti fauebiſ, fauebiſ &
mihi. Cum n̄. uiri boni & amici agit[ur]
reſ, reſ agitur noſtra. Vale.

Marſiliuſ ficinuſ laurentio medici Viro
magnanimo. Multi a te digniora ſe
petunt. Gregoriuſ epiphaniuſ longe dignio
e iiſ q̄ poſtulat. et ſi nobiſ amiciſſimuſ e͡t
tū ꝓ eiuſ uirtutem magiſ q̄ ꝓ amicitiā
eū. tibi comēdo. Nā ꝓ uirtutez eſt amicuſ.